CONGREGATIONAL

DANCING

IN

CHRISTIAN WORSHIP

CONGREGATIONAL

DANCING

IN

CHRISTIAN WORSHIP

by

DOUG ADAMS

THE SHARING COMPANY

Second Printing	1972
Third Printing	1972
Fourth Printing	1973
Fifth Printing	1974
Revised Edition	1976
Second Printing	1976
Revised Edition	1977
Revised Edition	1980
Second Printing	1984

a doxology

My special thanks to Margaret Chaney, who in-
spired me to undertake Congregational Dancing;
to Nicholas and Militsia Zernov, who taught me
that it is the height of Orthodox Christian
wisdom to dance; to Zalman Schachter, who
taught me to wiggle my toes even when stuck in
traffic on the lower deck of the Bay Bridge;
to Pat and Jo Sullivan, who shared a vision for
which to dance; to Sibby and Bridgett, my
college dance partners; to Bill Poteat, Anne
Scott, and Thomas Langford, who evoked me to
doing research and thinking on my own and gave
me time for the creative act to happen; to a
close friend Harvey Alper, who introduced me to
most of the above persons and who led me into
the habit of taking long walks; especially to
Harland Hogue and Wilhelm Wuellner and Durwood
Foster for giving me encouragement and guidance
to research, develop, and revise this book; to
Dan and Ginny Apra for allowing me to develop
congregational dancing at Arlington Church and
for dancing so full heartedly; to all the people
of College Heights Church for dancing so well;
To Gil, Dina, Mary, Dave, Sherry, Randolph,
Ron, Margit, Pearl, Schlomo, Dennis, Allen and
many other fellow dancers; and most of all to my
wife, Margo, who typed this work several times
in the process, and put up with weeks of my
preoccupation, and uplifts my spirits more than
dance or any person ever could. And finally to
my parents whose moral and financial support
made it possible for me to study leisurely in
school and not have to work through college and
seminary.

TABLE OF CONTENTS

TABLE OF CONTENTS CONTINUED

FOREWORD

This paper would guide the reader to understand
dancing through Ann Halprin's definition: the
"rhythmic phenomenon of the human being reacting
to his environment." As dance critic Jack
Anderson points out in Dance Magazine, such a
definition "is so broad that it could encompass
every human activity from being born to dying."[1]
From this modern perspective, sitting at·rest
as well as moving is an interaction with the
environment and hence qualifies as dancing.
Thus, there is already dancing in Christian
worship even if the congregation remains seated
throughout the worship or stands on only a few
occasions.

This new perspective carries us beyond a debate
cast in terms of whether or not there should be
dance in worship. From this new perspective we
see a new inquiry into whether the rudimentary
movements in present day Christian worship
services are consistent with and expressive of
the Christian liturgy or contradict it. The

---

1. "Ferment and Controversy," Dance Magazine,
August 1969, XLIII, 8, p. 48. Anna Halprin is
one of the leading figures in modern dance
theory and practice. Her roots and inspiration
spring from Jewish dance. She operates the
Dancers' Workshop in San Francisco.

question is no longer "Should there be dance in worship?" but rather "What dances (what movement) should be made during the different parts of the worship service so as to increase and not decrease the effect of liturgy?" For instance, there is a time to dance with joy in worship but probably not during the confession. There may be a time to sit and bow the head in sorrow and reflection but certainly not during the declaration of the good news or after the strengthening effects of communion!

This paper understands Christian worship as liturgy. The word "liturgy" comes from leitourgia which in the Greco-Roman world was the public work each person did to build and repair roads and bridges and other public works for the community and its growth. By calling their worship "liturgy", the early church pointed to the purpose for Christian worship to build roads and bridges among all peoples for the greater growth of community.

This paper combines a study of liturgy with a study of movement in Christian worship so that the words of liturgy will be forcefully incarnated: the Word will become flesh in our time in us. Of course, the words and movements of every liturgy vary; but each Christian worship

service should aim to produce certain effects
which the different dynamics of dance may aid.
After Chapter one briefly introduces the reader
to the different dynamics of dance, each subsequent chapter will explore in depth the theology and practice of dancing as such dancing
helps effect 1) all inclusive community with
equality, 2) complete repentance (the turning
away from preoccupation with self and the past),
3) fullest rejoicing, and 4) total rededication
to or reidentification with the tasks indicated
by the word liturgy. The preceding categories
are not mutually exclusive, nor is one sort of
dancing appropriate under only one category (for
instance, coming together in community and turning away from bondage to the past and self
results in rejoicing; rededication to the tasks
of liturgy helps strengthen community; etc.)
but rather the grouping is made to assist the
local minister or lay person locate easily the
movements which may heighten the effectiveness
of the worship service he or she is planning.
Because the focus of this study is on developing
principles and practices to guide ministers and
others to use dance in worship, the biblical and
theological materials are arranged throughout
the paper as they aid this development. Students
and scholars who are interested in dance materials from different perspectives or for different

purposes (for strictly biblical or theological discussions, etc.) will find this format disconcerting; but it is hoped that they will be able to gather insights for their study by a browsing of these chapters and that the bibliography will aid their search for works written in their area of interest. [2]

The theology in each section will be developed on the basis of linguistic, theological, psychological, literary, political, and historical insights offered by the Christian community itself. The practice in each section will reflect my own extended use of congregational dancing in worship services at Pacific School of Religion and Arlington Community Church as well as occasional use of dancing in direction of worship services for various conferences of the Northern California United Church of Christ, for several local churches within that conference for churches in Seattle, Phoenix and Washington D.C., and for my home church in Rockford, Ill.

---

2. The material is organized in historic progression and by different traditions in my booklet Involving People In Dancing Worship: Historic and Contemporary Patterns. (22pp. for $1.75 from The Sharing Company, P.O.Box 2224, Austin, Texas 78767), a useful study guide to this book for those tracing dance in particular periods or churches.

CHAPTER I

THE INTRODUCTORY STEPS

DANCING AND COMMUNITY

Let us begin where we find the members of our
congregations -- scattered in pews or chairs
throughout the nave. The pattern in which many
congregations seat themselves (if they are not
forced to sit together by lack of space) is
graphic confession in itself of our distance
from one another and from the table fellowship
of Christ. One may simply point out this distance as the confession and then read the
assurance and invite the people to move together
into front pews while they sing the processional
hymn. (The very lyrics of many of these hymns
suggest a moving together, e.g. "We Gather
Together.")

Most congregations find this first step an easy
one. Many congregations are accustomed to
having the minister and choir process during the
first hymn. One may observe that one reason so
many people fail to find community and joy in
worship is that instead of participating and
moving, they sit. Let the minister and choir

6

members admit that the sense of community and
joy they find in worship is due in part to their
greater involvement and movement together in
such activities as processions and recessions.

Introduction of biblical and early church
precedents for people processing will free many
people to participate. In biblical Hebrew, the
very word "company" is derived from "Dance." [3]
In the Psalms one is urged to come together to
praise the Lord with dancing. (Psalms 149 and
150). Much of David's success in building the
consciousness of community in early Israel and
unifying the tribes is attributed to his ability
in leading others in dance and communal celebration. His military successes have been
similarly attributed to the troupes' coordination
and espirit de corps attained through training
in dance. [4] (In modern day marches for peace

---

3. Mecholah translated "company" in Song of
Solomon 6.13 derives from mecholah which means
to dance with others in a group. In the wedding
ceremony pictured in this scriptural passage,
the two families processed toward each other to
symbolize that the marriage union of two would
lead to a wider union of all. R. deVaux, Ancient
Israel, (New York, 1961), p. 34.

4. C.H. Gordon, "David the Dancer," Yehezkel
Kaufmann Jubilee Volume,(Jerusalem, 1960),
pp. 46-49.

and racial justice, we have examples of the power of processions to evoke a sense of community and recommitment.) One points out that having all the people process to church singing hymns is an early church practice and was one means of gathering old and new members. [5]

Alternatively, if all the pews are filled at the start of the service, all or part of the congregation may be led in a procession down one aisle and up another or around the inside of the nave while all sing. On festive occasions the congregation or a part of it could process outside and around the church singing and perhaps even draw in a few bystanders as the early church did on the way to worship. [6] One may also have the congregation assemble outside the nave or chapel (in another room or outdoors) and then process into the nave singing the first hymn. [7]

5. The best account of people's processions from early days to the modern day is to be found in E. Louis Backman's Religious Dances, (London, 1952, passim.

6. Conducted at Skyline United Church, Oakland, California.

7. Conducted at worship for the Pastoral Conference at First Congregational Church, Berkeley, California, 1969.

If the congregation wishes to begin more innovative worship, they may wish to begin services
in the nave or chapel and then process singing
to the dining room (a most fitting room for
Christian worship) or some other location where
the worship could continue. [8] On such an
occasion one could well dispense with hymn books
and simply sing one chorus over and over again
('Chorus' means 'dance'). One should never
hesitate to sing the same song over and over
again nor to process around several times. One
needs to remember that Joshua, the man who led
the tribes into the promised land, had the
people process around the city of Jericho seven
times before taking it. In the same way, we
need to spend time readying our people for the
work of worship so that they will enter into it
in the proper spirit.

Sometime after the people have moved forward
into the front pews (or gathered in one of the
preceding ways) the time comes for the Lord's
prayer. One may aid the understanding and effect
of the prayer by simply having the people join
hands and raise them up as they pray the "Our
Father." much of the individualism which has

---

8. Conducted at Second Congregational Church,
Rockford, Illinois.

developed in our society has been traced to the
lack of ceremonial in Protestant worship. [9]
Let us confess that many pray and understand the
Lord's Prayer as if it were "My Father." Holding hands and raising them while praying "Our
Father" aids the realization of the prayer's
intent to draw us into community and incarnational concern for others and to bring the kingdom on earth.

The foregoing should give a taste of the community producing dynamic of dance and its
possibilities for \Christian worship. This
dynamic and its practical applications for producing particular patterns of community will be
explored in much greater detail in chapter two.

DANCING AND REPENTANCE

A second dynamic which dancing helps produce is
repentance. As noted earlier, repentance is
here understood as a turning away from preoccupation with self and the past. Evelyn
Underhill has noted the loss of self-preoccupation
that occurs in dance and likens such a sacrifice

---

9. S. F. Winward, The Reformation of Our Worship,
(Richmond, 1964), particularly "Embodied Worship," pp. 53-73.

as similar to the one that must occur in the
religious rite. [10] In his sermon "On Repentance"
St. Ambrose calls by the word "dance" the similar
process of shaking off preoccupation with
thoughts about the past so as to free one to
face the present and make the future:

> St. Paul danced in the spirit when he ex-
> erted himself for us, when he endeavored
> to be a soldier of Christ, because he
> forgot the past and longed for the fut-
> ure. [11]

We should convey the foregoing insights to the
people whom we have gathered in the front pews
of our church. Then we can lead them in two
simple dance sequences to aid this self-sacrifice
which will prepare all to better attend to the
gospel and exposition of God's word. The
following sequence, which this author has used
in many churches, also aids in demonstrating how
much more meaning is conveyed by incarnating
the words.

First the minister says to the congregation and

---

10. Evelyn Underhill, Worship,(New York,1957)
p. 53.
11. St. Ambrose, "On Repentance," Patrologia
Latina, Migne, ed., (Paris, 1857), Vol. 16, col.
1180, Eng. trans. Backman, op. cit., p. 26.

has them repeat the following lines from Paul's
letter to the Romans 12.1:

    Minister: "I appeal to you brethren by the
                  mercies of God. . .
    People: "I appeal to you brethren by the
                  mercies of God. . .
    Minister: ". . . to present your bodies as
                  a living sacrifice."
    People: ". . . to present your bodies as
                  a living sacrifice."

The minister then repeats the foregoing sequence
incorporating movements. One spreads one's arms
to a wide open position as he says: "I appeal to
you brethren by the mercies of God." The
congregation imitiates the movement as they
repeat the same line. Then the minister rises
while lifting the arms slightly saying, "to
present your bodies as a living sacrifice."
The congregation imitates this movement as they
repeat the line. All are now on their feet and
prepared for more movement.

Ray Repp has written a song which lends itself
to developing this repentance dynamic further.
The title is "Into Your Hands." [12] The song is

12. Ray Repp, "Songs From Come Alive," F.E.L.
Song Book, IV, (Chicago, 1967), pp. 4-5. I am
grateful to David and Sherry Atkins and Richard
Corson for developing this choreography.

written in the traditional stanza-chorus signification -- a signification which results
from early church choreography. "Stanza" means
stand or halt; "chorus" means dance. In the
church the people would stand in position while
a soloist or choir sang or danced the stanza;
but then during the chorus, all the people would
begin to move. In using "Into Your Hands" one
may teach the people the following movement for
the chorus and have a soloist or choir dance the
stanza. (Or one may simply teach the chorus
movement to the people with the intervening
stanza simply sung by all or left out altogether).

The chorus could be taught to the congregation
in the fashion suggested earlier for teaching
the movement to the scripture -- lining it out
(singing one line and having the congregation
sing it back, then the next line and so on).
Then all sing the chorus through in its entirety.
Finally, one adds the following movements. While
singing "Into Your Hands we commend our spirits
O Lord," one extends ones hands and arms out
toward the people in oblation. While singing
"Into your hands we commend our hearts," one
brings the hands to the chest in a position of
concentration. While singing "For we must die
to ourselves in loving you," one bends at the
waist as one's arms sweep to the floor in a deep

bowing motion. While singing "Into your hands we commend our love," one repeats the first motion of extending one's hands and arms out toward the people.

Some may not be physically able to follow in all these motions; but they should be invited to do whatever is within their capacity. Some elderly women in wheel chairs have been able to do a semblance of these actions with their arms and have had a moving experience.

Some churches may postpone the active congregational participation and prefer to introduce dance into worship through a dance choir. The sacrificial dynamic of dance should lead us to the opposite action. Without some congregational participation, the congregation sits and often becomes critical. When one sits, one is likely to see this or that distraction; but when one becomes involved and dances, one is much less likely to become fixated on any detail and so is much less critical. If a dance choir is to be used, one should have the congregation sing a chorus or clap along. The dance choir is less likely to be self-conscious if it is leading the congregation and not just performing.

This sacrificial dynamic of dance was impressed

14

upon me by a photograph which was one of forty
taken of our dance group at Pacific School of
Religion. On the way to seminary, I had rolled
up my sleeves. On arrival in the chapel, I had
neglected to roll them down. Everyone was so
involved in the dancing that no one's attention
was distracted by my naked arms. The photog-
rapher was singing along with the music; and so
even he did not have his attention drawn away
from the central thrust of the dance by the minor
detail.

During the "Into Your Hands" choreography just
outlined, some people may brush others, expecially in the bowing gesture. So that no one
feels self-conscious about this contact, one
could say at the close of this exercise that
naturally we brush into others in our worship,
for we are not alone. By such contact we are
reminded of our togetherness. Some incarnational
theology could be introduced at this point with
the passing of the peace. Thus people will see
that repentance leads to a more complete sense
of community through interaction with others.

While the people are still standing, it is time
for the gospel reading. If people are seated,
one might invite them to stand for the gospel.
a major reason for the preceding sacrifice or

repentance is to prepare our minds to attend to the gospel. Shaking off preoccupation with self and the past is for the purpose of making us ready to sense the intention of God's will for the present and future. Most Christians throughout the world stand as the gospel is read. This standing is not only a sign of respect but also a way to prepare the people's minds to attend to the message. To better prepare themselves in Coptic churches, the people dance before the gospel is read. [13] Other aspects of this repentance dynamic and practice of dance will be explored in greater detail in chapter three.

DANCING AND REJOICING

The gospel to be shared when introducing dance is Luke 6.23: "Rejoice and leap for joy." In Aramaic which Jesus spoke, the word for "rejoice" is the word for "dance." [14] Dance was the means for coming back to joy as well as expressing it; hence, "leap for joy." He probably said simply "Rejoice!" for a Jew would understand that dance was the way to "rejoice."

13. C.F.Rey, The Real Abyssinia,(London), p.190.
14. Matthew Black, The Aramaic Approach to the Gospel and Acts, (London, 1967), p. 158.

That dance was understood by Jews as being the
means to rejoice at the time of Jesus is suggested by a comparison of Matthew 5.12 and
Luke 6.23:

> Blessed are ye, when men shall revile you,
> and persecute you, and shall say all manner
> of evil against you falsely, for my sake.
> Rejoice, and be exceedingly glad; for great
> is your reward in heaven; for so they perse-
> cuted the prophets which were before you.
> (Matthew 5.11-12)

> Blessed are ye, when men shall hate you, and
> when they shall separate you from their com-
> pany, and shall reproach you, and cast out
> your name as evil, for the Son of man's
> sake. Rejoice ye in that day, and <u>leap for
> joy</u>: for, behold, your reward is great in
> heaven; for in a like manner did their
> fathers unto the prophets.
> (Luke 6.22-23)

The underlining is added to call attention to
the chief difference we will consider in the
two records. As usual Luke makes explicit to
the Greek mind what would be inplicitly understood from Matthew by the Jew. This understanding (rejoice = dance) lies behind many scriptural passages and translations and supports the
coherency of the lyrics in many of our hymns as
we will note in chapter four along with the
fund of choreographies thus suggested.

One chorus that is appropriately titled to convey

this dynamic of dance is "Happy is the Man who walks in the Way of the Lord:"

> Happy are people who walk in the way of the Lord our God and King
> Happy are they and Blessed are they that put their trust in God
> Sing Hosanna Halleluia. 15

A lining out of this song with the congregation in the fashion suggested earlier may be aided by an alteration in the lyric. One should repeat the first line instead of using the second line. Thus the chorus is made easier for people to remember, and the people are freed to enter fully into the procession. The minister or choir lead all who wish to process around and around the outer aisles of the nave and end up moving down the center of the nave to the altar for a final dedication or offering. All in the church sing the hymn whether they process or remain standing in the pews.

To bring the whole body into play, one may invite people to clap or jingle their keys as they sing. Clapping is a perfectly biblical activity in worship. Psalm 47 says "Clap your hands together, all you people. Oh sing unto God

---

15. Repp, op. cit., pp. 12-13.

with the voice of melody." In the history of
the church, hand clapping has often accompanied
singing. In the early church, the people even
applauded the minister's sermon. [16] We ministers hate to think why the people have given up
that practice!

DANCING AND REDEDICATION

The final dynamic of dancing to be explored in
this study resides in the power it has to help
effect a rededication to or reidentification
with the work of God in the community. This
dynamic has been outlined earlier in connection
with the community producing effect of marching.
The power of this dynamic may be utilized in the
most traditional worship services during the
recessional hymn. As all joined in the processing so all may join in recessing. The
recessing may be done in different ways to
emphasize the particular message for the day.
(The complications of having hymnals in hands
may be eliminated by having the recessional be
one verse of a familiar hymn sung over and over
again -- thus the people are freed to look up
and around at each other.)

---

16. Fred C. Conybeare, Philo About the Contemplative Life, (Oxford, 1895), pp. 253ff.

If the emphasis is on community, one may have
the people exit two by two holding hands. The
third stanza of "In Christ There Is No East or
West" ("join hands then family of the faith") is
perfect for this sort of recession as is the
second stanza of "They'll Know We Are Christians
By Our Love" ("we will walk with each other we
will walk hand in hand") [17] If recessing is
impossible, then people may join hands in the
pews while singing these stanzas; but the sense
of intention is greatly increased by walking out
together.

If the message is that of hope in spite of
recent setbacks, one may have the people go
forth singing "Amen" or "Ain't Gonna Let Nobody
Turn Me Round." [18] The message may be height-
ened by having the people do the tripudium step
(which means "three step" or "jubilate" in
Latin and which is simply three steps forward
and one back, three steps forward and one back,
etc.) Clapping of hands with the steps helps to
keep people moving together. "Forward Through
the Ages" sung to the tune of "Onward Christian
Soldiers" is a familiar recessional that

17. Hymnal For Young Christians, (Chicago, 1968),
pp. 74-75
18. Guy Carawan, ed., We Shall Overcome: Songs
of the Southern Freedom Movement, (New York,
1963), pp. 60-61.

reemphasizes the ongoingness of the community.

The _tripudium_ step was the most common dance step
in Christian church processions for a thousand
years and fits with any hymns of 2/4, 3/4, or
4/4 time. Most significantly the people did
this step not in single file or in circle dances;
but rather they did it in processions with many
abreast with arms linked in row after row --
moving through the streets and into the church
and around in it during the hymns of the service
and then out through the streets as a recessional.
(Moving three or five or ten or more abreast
makes the doing of this step much easier -- one
can hardly fall behind.) And this manner of
dance, which has the character of a march that
does not simply go in circles, is in keeping
with a faith that believes in history and not
cyclical ways in the world. Taking three steps
forward and one back, three steps forward and
one back leads to an optimistic spirit that sees
set backs in the context of ongoing progress.
Further discussion of this rededication dynamic
will be explored in chapter five.

Hopefully, all of the foregoing practices will
help the people to see our God as an active,
moving God who calls us to a life together that

affirms the material world as good and affirms worship as a part of history -- a time in which we work to upbuild God's Kingdom on earth.

CHAPTER II

DANCING AND COMMUNITY

Congregational dancing in Christian worship has
aided the development of particular patterns or
qualities of Christian community: 1) a kind of
community where moving toward God is moving
with and toward other people; and 2) a kind of
community where all persons are included as
equals. Where congregational dancing has flour-
ished in Christian worship, these qualities of
community have tended to develop. Suppression
of congregational dancing has often been accompanied by a decline in these qualities of
community; and such a suppression of dancing has
often been expressly pursued to eliminate these
qualities. Let us explore the connection of
dancing with each quality of community and then
outline some practical congregational movements
to achieve each of these qualities in present
day Christian worship.

MOVING TOWARD GOD AND OTHER PEOPLE

The kind of dancing affirmed in Jewish and
Christian worship effects the realization that
our coming to God includes a coming together with

other people in community. First we will survey
the Jewish and Christian records and see that
communal rather than individual dancing is the
norm for worship; then we will explore the
effects of communal and individual dancing to
see why the former is preferable to the latter
and other less corporate ways of coming to God;
and finally we will propose corporate ways of
dancing for our time.

OLD TESTAMENT AND JEWISH EVIDENCE

A survey of the instances of dance in the Old
Testament (outlined in a schema as appendix one)
suggests that there was no individual dance to
God in pure Israelite practice. The group dance
was normative in worship as we will see below
in discussing first the group and then the individual dances reported in the Old Testament.
This paper does not contend that that communal
dance was always a dance to God, but rather that
when dance was used in Israelite worship such
dance took the communal form.

The principle word for dance in the Old Testament
is in its various forms Machol, mecholah, and
and chul (chul being the infinitive). These
forms denote the same group circle dances and
are translated by χορός in the Greek Septuagint
and chorea in the Latin Vulgate. These words

mean that the dance was by a group circling
rather than by an individual. [19] (In this
group dancing, movements by the individuals
could be either wild or graceful. As we will
see, the tendency in Jewish circles has been to
accept a wide range of even awkward individual
movements within the group; but the priestly
traditions in both the Jewish and Christian
circles have tended to impose standards of some
individual grace or at least group harmony in
such dancing.)

The communal nature of this dance is explicitly
stated in cases where worship is involved, as
in Psalm 149.3: "Let them praise his name with
dancing." In the very picture of God's heavenly
restoration of Zion is this communal dancing:
"Go forth in the dances of them that make merry"
(Jeremiah 31.4), and "Then shall the virgin rejoice in the dance, both young men and old together ..." (Jeremiah 31.13).

This communal dancing in worship is true to the
earliest prophetic practices, the later Talmudic

---

19. Julian Morgenstern, "The Etymological History
of the Three Hebrew Synonyms for 'To Dance'."
American Oriental Society Journal, 36, (1916),
pp. 321-332.

26

and Midrashic vision of man's coming to God, and
the whole history of Hebraic practice. The
early prophetic practice is reported in I Samuel
10.5 where dancing is carried out in a band.
W.O.E. Oesterley points out that the word for
'band' (hebel) means rope which suggests the
connectedness of those dancing. [20] A vision of
heaven throughout Talmud and Midrash includes
the communal dance:

> R. Berekiah and R. Helbo and Ulla Bira'ah
> of beri and R. Eleazar said in the name of
> R. Hanina: in the Time To Come, the Holy
> One Blessed be He, will lead the chorus
> (holah) of the righteous ... and they will
> dance around him ... and point to Him, as
> it were with a finger, saying, This is God,
> our God forever and ever; He will lead
> us ... with youthfulness, with liveliness.
> [21]

---

20. W.O.E. Oesterley, The Sacred Dance. (New
York, 1923) p. 108.

21. H. Freedman and Maurice Simon, ed., The
Midrash, (London, 1939), IV, trans. J. Israel-
stan, "Shemini" (Leviticus) XI. 9, p. 151.
Rabbi Hanina bar Hama, a student of Rabbi, was
in the first generation of Amoraim (A.D. 219-
257). This same story is repeated in the
Midrash, ibid., IX, trans. Maurice Simon, "Song
of Songs," VII. I:2, p. 277. Similar stories
are associated with 1) R. Jose bar Hanina of the
second generation of Amoraim (A.D. 257-300):
The Midrash on Psalms, trans. William G. Braude,
(New Haven, 1959), 9. 463; and 2) R. Eleazar
ben Pedath of the third generation Amoraim (A.D.
300-330):   (continued next page)

Israel Abrahams asserts that throughout Jewish
History the shape of dances has been conditioned
by the desire to have all caught up in the
community:

> Dancing, however, was not so much a personal
> pleasure as a means of rousing the enthusi-
> asm of the assembled company. Hence
> gesticulations, violent leaps and bounds,
> hopping in a circle, rather than graceful
> pose or soft rhythmic movement, character-
> ized the Jewish Dances both of ancient and
> medieval times   22

The foregoing examination of Israelite dance
supports Abraham's assertion of the communal
means and goal of Jewish dancing.

As is evident from a survey of appendix one,
there are only a few exceptions to communal

---

21. (cont.) I. Epstein, ed., The Talmud, (London,
1938), trans., J. Rabbinowitz, "Ta'anith 31a,
Mo'ed VII, pp. 164-5. Other rabbis conveying
this vision are R. Ulla bar Ishmael of beri
(Bira'ach) of the second generation of Amoraim,
and R. Helbo and R. Berekiah of the fourth generation of Amoraim. For background and dating
of these rabbis and their work, see Hermann L.
Strack's Introduction to the Talmud and Midrash,
(Philadelphia, 1931), supplemented by material
from "Excursus III", by H. Loewe in his Rabbinic
Anthology (New York, 1938).
22. Israel Abrahams, Jewish Life in the Middle
Ages, (New York, 1896), p. 380.

dance in the Old Testament. These exceptions
are less surely dancing to God. Chief among
these individual dances is David's dance called
karrar in 2 Sammuel 6.14 and 16 and raqad in
I Chronicles 15.29. These are translated
όρχοὐυενος in the Greek and saltatio in the
Latin and indicate an individual circling and
jumping. Some of the scholarship on David's
dance identifies this dance not exclusively as
a dance to God or even primarily as that, but
rather as a prelude to his coronation as king
and accompanying sexual union with Michal. [23]
J. R. Porter's article connecting 2 Samuel 6
and Psalm 132 offers interesting although involved
arguments that this event of David's dance was
a coronation ritual celebrated within the
Jerusalem cultus. [24] That David's dance was
also connected to the sexual rites with Michal
which would be expected to consumate the coronation does not necessarily follow as Porter
seems too readily to assume. But as Porter notes
elimination of much of 2 Samuel 6 in the later
priestly account (I Chronicles 15.29) could

---

23. J. R. Porter, "An Interpretation of 2 Samuel
VI and Psalm CXXXII," The Journal of Theological
Studies, V(1954), pp. 161-173.
24. For additional information on this cultus,
see Aubrey Johnson, "The Role of the King in the
Jerusalem Cultus," The Labyrinth, S.H.Hooke, ed.
(London, 1935), pp. 73-111.

indicate that the priests saw at least a suggestion of sexual practice and wished to eliminate
it. [25] But David's dance may be seen as in line
with the dance of the prophets with whom he is
seen dancing earlier. Michal's anger at seeing
him dance would then be understandable; for the
prophets opposed the power of her father Saul.
At the very moment when David should be coming
to her to continue the line of Saul, David does
a dance showing his loyalty to the prophetic.
The few other instances of the use of raqad
refer to a dance in Isaiah 13.21 by satyrs
(certainly not divine) and material in Job and
Ecclesiastes. These latter two books stress an
individual orientation alien to the basic Jewish
spirit. The dance described in Job 21.11 and
Ecclesiastes 3.4 is in keeping with the self-
centered orientation of these books but certainly
not with the mainstream of Israelite thinking and
practice. The orientation of these books is the

---

25. R. Abba b. Kahana (c.A.D. 275) identifies
David's dance with a very sexual kind and sides
with Michal in criticizing David for dancing in
such a way: The Midrash, op. cit., V trans. J.
Slotki, "Bemidbar" IV. 20 (Numbers), p. 135.
Other rabbis continued in the reaction of the
writers of I Chronicles in reducing the dance to
"he turned the front of his foot" and explain
David's nakedness by "he stood on tiptoe, revealing his naked toes.""Bemindbar," ibid., p. 133.

very thing which Israelite dance strives to overcome. [26]

NEW TESTAMENT AND CHRISTIAN EVIDENCE

In view of the foregoing, the Christian Church acted true to the deepest understanding of Jewish tradition in supporting in worship as it did the group dance (<u>chorea</u> or χορός), while suppressing the individual dance (<u>saltatio</u> or ὀρχούμενος). We will examine this pattern of Church action after seeing how New Testament evidence of dancing supports this thesis that coming to God in dance includes coming to and with others.

The group dance (χορός) accompanies the return of the son to his father (Luke 15.25). This return of son to father is paradigmatic for our worship; and the inclusion of the χορός kind

---

26. Of course it is not the purpose of this book to prove that the orientations of Ecclesiastes and Job are alien to the Jewish spirit. It must suffice here to note that the sense of community (in its historical dimensions) would eliminate the sense of futility portrayed in Ecclesiastes and the sense of injustice portrayed in Job. The complaints in these two books result from reflecting on the fate of the individual and not the community.

of dancing in this scene is supportive of our
thesis.

The references to individual dancing (ὀρχούμενος
in the New Testament are in connection with
decidedly nonworshipful scenes. The dance of
Salome before Herod is of this kind. (Matthew
14.6 and Mark 6.22). The remaining instance of
dancing is also of this kind; but this instance
requires careful attention because the passage
which includes this dancing has often been mis-
read as Jesus' call for individual dance. [27]
In Matthew 11.17 and Luke 7.32 occurs this
passage:

> And the Lord said, Whereunto then shall I
> liken the men of this generation? And to
> what are they like? They are like unto the
> children sitting in the marketplace, and
> calling to one another and saying, We have
> piped unto you, and ye have not danced; we
> have mourned to you, and ye have not wept.
> For John the Baptist came neither eating
> bread nor drinking wine; and ye say, He
> hath a devil. The Son of Man is come
> eating and drinking; and ye say, Behold a
> gluttonous man, and a winebibber, a friend
> of publican and sinners! (Luke 7.31-34).

------

27. Ambrose misreads this passage in this way:
St. Ambrose, "On Repentance," op. cit., p. 26,
Eng. trans. Backman, op. cit., p. 26.

In the preceding passage, Christ is not calling
for the people to dance individual dances;
rather "this generation" acted like the children
in the marketplace expecting such a performance.
This passage deals not with a call to individual
dance but rather with false expectations and the
resulting errors in judging others. From the
concluding verses it is obvious that John the
Baptist does not fulfill the dancing expectation
and Jesus does not fulfill the weeping one.

In Eastern Orthodoxy this distinction between
the group dance (χορός) and the individual
dance (ὀρχούμενος), with support of the former
and suppression of the latter, is clearly continued. For example, Gregory of Nazianzus,
(A.D. 329-388) "The Theologian" of the Eastern
Orthodox Church and Bishop of Constantinople,
advised the people that doing triumphant ring
dances (χορός) was the proper way to celebrate
Easter; [28] but he cautioned the emperor against
individual dance of the kind done by the daughter
of Herod. [29] In similar fashion, another of

---

28. Chr. Bromel, Fest-Tantze der ersten Christen,
(Jena, 1701), Eng. trans., Backman, op.cit.,p. 31.
29. Gregory of Nazianzus, "Against Julianus II,"
Patrologia Graeca (hereafter P. Gr.), Migne, ed.,
(Paris, 1857), Vol. 35, col. 710, Eng. trans.
Backman, op.cit., p. 31. Gregory advises that if
the emperor must do individual dances at least
let him do one in the spirit of David whom Gregory
considers to have approached God.

"the doctors" of the Eastern Church, Basil the Great (A.D. 344-407), Bishop of Caesarea, urged his people to perform the ring dance (χορός); [30] but Basil attacked individual dance (ὀρχούμενος) done by some women, for such dancing distracted the attention of the men who sat and watched in church. [31] Yet another of "the doctors" of Orthodoxy, John Chrysostom (A.D. 345-407), Bishop of Constantinople, blessed the performance of the ring dances (χορός); but censored those who through excess engaged in the individual dance (ὀρχούμενος). [32] One is given feet for comely ring dances: [33] but one should refrain from the unbridled dance [34] or the camel sort of dance (ὀρχούμενος). [35]

---

30. Basil, "Epistle ad. I,2," Migne, P.Gr., ibid., Vol. 32, col. 226, Eng. trans., Backman, op. cit., p. 25.

31. "Sermon on Drunkeness," Num. I, Migne, P.Gr., Ibid. Vol. 31, col. 446, 459. Eng. trans. Backman, op. cit., p. 25. Even worse, such women join with others and desecrate even the group dance (χορός).

32. John Chrysostom, "On the Resurrection of Lazarus," I, Migne, P.Gr., Ibid., Vol 48, col 963. Eng. trans., Backman, Op. cit., p. 32.

33. "hom. ad Agricolas," Bromel, op. cit., Eng. trans., Backman, op. cit., p. 33.
34. "Sermon on Marriage," Migne, P.Gr., op. cit., p. 32.
35. "Commentary on the Gospel of St. Matthew," 48, Migne, P.Gr., Vol. 58, col. 492, Eng. trans., Backman, op. cit., p. 32.

In Western Catholicism, where invading hoards of pagans threatened to overwhelm the church, all forms of people's participation were restricted including dance. But even in the West, the chorea continued to command respect -- albeit in a highly symbolic form. While Ambrose (A.D. 340-397), bishop of Milan, had praised bodily dance, [36] his student Augustine (A.D. 354-430), writing in a more chaotic period, encouraged the people and the church to understand the dance of Psalms 149.3 and 150.4 in an exclusively symbolic way:

> Let them praise His Name in chorus (ver.3). What meaneth "chorus"? Many know what a "chorus" is; nay, as we are speaking in a town, almost all know. A "chorus" is the union of singers. If we sing "in chorus", let us sing in concord. ...The whole world is now the chorus of Christ. The chorus of Christ soundeth harmoniously from east to west. 37

Of course, the Hebrew language, of which Augustine was ignorant, suggests that dance does lead to a sense of company as we have already explored; but the Hebrews recognized the need

---

36. Ambrose, "Commentary on Psalm 118," Migne, P.L., op. cit., Vol. 15, col. 1290, Eng. trans., Backman, op. cit., p. 30.
37. Augustine, "Exposition of Psalms," The Nicene and Post Nicene Fathers, first series, 8, (New York, 1888), p. 678.

for all the people to dance literally with all
their might to achieve this end of community.
As we will see in the next section of this paper,
The Catholic Hierarchy knew all too well the
power of literal group dance. The Catholic objection to popular participation in dance reveals
a political dimension of dancing. The superior
position which clergy in the Catholic church
maintained over their laity had required that
dancing together be suppressed as too equalizing
and revolutionary. Into this century there is
approval only of dancing which will not "get
out of hand." [38]

Thus, the Catholic hierarchy had officially
sanctioned only an aesthetic use and understanding of dance in connection with the mass. "Los
seises," the six dancing choir boys in the
Mozarabe mass in Seville received papal sanction.
[39] And official publications as well as noted
individual catholics have described the mass as

---

38. "Dancing," The Catholic Encyclopedia, (New
York, 1908), Vol. 4, pp. 618-619.

39. "A Bull of Pope Eugene IV of 1439 authorizes
the dances of 'los seises,'" Backman, op.cit.,
p. 78.

a dance in slow motion. [40]

THE EFFECT OF COMMUNAL DANCING

Having communal dancing in worship is important
so that we do not develop an irreconcilable
stress between responding to God and living in
community. Of course worship does attempt to
create a tension between the present conditions
of community and the gifts and demands of God
so as to stimulate our action; but our worship
must be corporate so that the resolution of this
tension is sought in corporate action and improv-
ment rather than through individual withdrawal.
For instance, many of the practices of religion
(particularly the mental ways of meditation) may
lead the person to look upon other people,
community and one's own body as bad because such
mental meditation fosters a stillness which can
be disturbed by later activities necessitated
by material life and life with others; and

---

40. D. Attwater, ed., A Catholic Dictionary,
(New York, 1962). Earlier in this century this
description of the mass as dance was given by
Monsignor Robert Hugh Benson, Papers of A Pariah,
(London, 1909). Jacques Maritain has similarly
described the mass: Art and Scholasticism,
(New York, 1930), trans. J.F. Scanlow, p. 56.
Ronald Knox elaborated this description in The
Mass In Slow Motion, (New York, 1948).

thus one could come to see the relationship with
God as opposed by the demands of community and
could withdraw from community. In contrast to
mental practices and their result, dance includes
body movement which later activity in life does
not disturb but rather continues; and so, one
is led to see the secular in the sacred -- all
caught up in one. These dynamics as well as
the ones discussed earlier in relation to dance
and the creation of community should help us
understand Gerhardus van der Leeuw's suggestion
that the separation that leads one to distinguish
sacred from profane arises only as the dance
diminishes; and the reemergence of the dance is
likely to sweep away separations that the critical
minded person creates by sitting and not
dancing. [41]

As dance is preferable to less corporate ways
of meditation so that one comes to look upon
activity and material life as consistent with
response to God, so communal dance is preferable
to individual dance so that one comes to look
upon the constraints of living in community as
a part of the response to God: a condition one
should accept and not an evil one should try
to escape.

41. Gerhardus van der Leeuw, Sacred and Profane
Beauty:The Holy in Art, (New York,1963), passim.

COMMUNAL DANCES FOR TODAY

In chapter one we detailed several ways of communal dancing to help develop a consciousness that moving toward God is moving with and toward other people. (All people processing forward while singing the first hymn at the beginning of the worship service aids this understanding. Also holding others' hands while praying the Lord's Prayer helps many to understand this dynamic of our faith. Both practices could be introduced with some of the foregoing material to aid in the development of this understanding.) Let us explore several other simple ways to effect this understanding through movements which are appropriate in the standard Sunday morning worship and then examine more involved ways which are appropriate to more innovative worship (although from the standpoint of the history of dance in worship which we have briefly surveyed, innovative worship services with corporate dance may be judged much more traditional than the standard Sunday morning worship of most churches.)

As people hold hands while praying the Lord's Prayer, so they may join hands while saying the creed to emphasize their solidarity. [42]

42. Donald Postema leads his congregation in this practice in Ann Arbor, Michigan.

A modification of having the people hold hands
while praying the Lord's Prayer is having the
people move forward to a position around the
communion table while they are praying the
Lord's Prayer. Thus we graphically see that our
approach to God includes our approach to others.
When the people gather around the table, they
should be encouraged to form a circle taking
each other by the hand and lifting up their
hands and arms to signify the strength and joy
we gain from our relationship to God and each
other and to signify our task to uplift the
world.

Moving forward with others to the communion
table while praying may strike some as a strange
attitude of prayer. Many in our time are accustomed to think that the proper attitude for
Christian prayer is to close the eyes, bow the
head, while sitting in the pew. First century
Christians would find such sitting posture very
strange indeed! The rows of pews (which in
early Christianity were few in number and re-
served for the aged and infirm) would be viewed
as a sad testimony to the vitality of Christianity in the West today. [43]

---

[43]. Worship without pews is still carried on in
most Eastern Orthodox churches -- although many
in America have allowed pews to the distress of
many defenders of the faith. Nicholas Zernov,
Orthodox Encounter, (London, 1961), p. 53.

As Gerhard Delling has shown through Old and New
Testament study, the standard Jewish and early
Christian position of prayer was standing.
Special conditions of privation or severe agi-
tation on occasion led to an attitude of prayer
on one's knees close to prostration. [44] Thus
during the confession, one might kneel; but
during the Lord's Prayer one's sense of close-
ness to God should certainly lead to the standing
position. The Lord's command to "rise and pray"
(Luke 22.46) should be taken seriously by us
all to increase our attention to God's will.
As we are instructed, "I will therefore that men
pray everywhere, lifting up holy hands, without
wrath and doubting." (I Timothy 2.8).

Having the people moving forward around the
communion table while praying the Lord's Prayer
brings them into position for communion. Another

---

44. Gerhard Delling, "Prayer," Worship in the New
Testament," (London, 1962, pp. 104-108.) The
Puritans in America always stood for prayer,
with arms raised above their heads, for they
followed Biblical pattern in much of worship
where the Biblical pattern was clear. Some Puritans noted that dance in worship would be appropriate (as the Bible notes dance in worship);
but lacking the church history to know what
dances were meant by the Bible, the Puritans advised against dancing in worship until such
history was known.

way to bring people into the proper position for
communion is to have the people approach the
table with at least one other person in hand. [45]
This method helps people realize the thrust of
Jesus' saying that alone one does not approach
Christ: "For where two or three are gathered
together in my name there am I in the midst
of them," (Matthew 18.20).

The way we celebrate communion and the other
sacraments alters the effect they may have on
the people. For instance, the effects of communion toward developing a communal consciousness may be greatly lessened if the people eat
separate little pieces of bread or drink from
separate little cups in pews while facing others'
backs! One need not belabor these points further. One should celebrate communion so as to
reinforce the effects intended. Bringing the
people forward around the altar or around several tables set up in the nave will probably
require more time than serving the people in the
pews; [46] but the length of the sermons could

----

45. J. Hood Snavely and his United Church of
Christ in Woodside, Calif., approach communion
this way.
46. Conducted at the Pastoral Conference, 1st
Congregational Church, Berkeley, 1970, based on
the early Reformation Scotch Presbyterian
pattern.

be cut somewhat to allow the time for a communion
that will foster community and not just individualism. [47]

For more flexible worship service, Margaret
Taylor has choreographed "No Man Is An Island,"
which is perfectly suited to aid the understanding we would develop: [48]

> "No man is an island, no man stands alone,"
> Everyone moves about freely in all direct-
> ions, but looking toward one person and
> then another, spontaneously.
> "Each man's joy ..." Each one stands and
> thrusts arms up vertically and smiles. In
> this upward stretch, the fingers are ex-
> tended.
> "Is joy to me." Each one, with arms held
> high, rushes to join spontaneously with
> whoever is nearby to form small groups of
> three, four, five, or six persons. As
> persons cluster in these groups, the
> fingertips of their right hands touch high
> center together. It seems as if the right
> hands have been like magnets that drew
> nearby person into these clusters.
> "Each man's grief is my own." Remaining
> in the small group he has just joined,

---

47. Similarly if a font of stagnant water (instead of a stream or a fountain of flowing
water) is used to baptize a child with a few
drops of water, something of the dramatic effec-
ting of interrelation with all the world is lost
and the symbolic foundation for a sense of responsibility for mission in the world is gone.
48. Taylor, Creative Movement, p. 10. Change
"man" to "one" for inclusive language.

each participant now reaches in compassion
with his left hand to touch the shoulder
of the person directly ahead of him. The
right hands that have been touching high
in the center remain touching but lower to
shoulder level.
"We need one another." Each one steps back,
and the group forms a simple circle with
the joining of hands. All look around at
one another with friendly smiles.
"So I will defend ..." During the first
two words, each person swings his right
hand into the center close enough that all
palms overlap. Then during the second two
words, the left hands are brought center and
the left palms stack up on top of the pile
of right palms, thus symbolizing a pledge
of mutual commitment.
"Each man as my brother." During the first
two words each person's arms swing up and
spread out wide to rest on the adjacent
persons' arms held shoulder high, so that
everyone is linked together as in a Zorba
dance. During the singing of "as my
brother" the group can sway to the right,
or everyone in the group can take three
steps to the right, and of course everyone
looks across at the others smiling.
"Each man as my friend." Holding the same
arm position, everyone can sway back to the
left or take three steps to the left.
However, they should avoid looking down at
their feet. They should, instead, look
around at one another, smiling, for this
is the time of celebration of the brotherhood of man. "By this all men will know
that you are my disciple, if you have love
for one another." (John 13.35).

Many of the choreographies originally designed
by Margaret Taylor and others for rhythmic
choirs may now be adapted for congregational

44

participation. [49] Those dances based on
carols are particularly appropriate for developing this communal sense, for to carol is
to dance; and the lyrics of many carols call
for movement. [50]

Numerous educational techniques developed by
Esalen and other retreat centers may be adapted
for innovative worship to develop a communal
sense. The crepe paper walk is particularly
valuable in worship to help people see constraints of communal life as a worthwhile part
of life not always to be broken. That we need

49. Margaret Taylor, Time for Discovery,(Boston,
1964). See also Violet Bruce and Joan Tooke, Lord
of the Dance: An Approach to Religious Education,
(London, 1966). An indispensable source for
suggestions of this kind is The Sacred Dance
Guild Journal which reports in detail all the
dance activity in worship, state by state three
times a year. (Available from "Sacred Dance Guild"
c/o Susan Cole, 3917 N.E. 44 St., Vancouver,
Washington 98661. $16 per year but $8 for students.)

50. Suzanne Aker, "To Carol is to Dance," Dance
Magazine, December, 1964, pp. 40-41. For background see also M. Sahlin's Etude sur las carole
medieval(Uppsala 1940) and W. Sandy's Carols
Ancient and Modern, (London, 1833). For carols
themselves see Vaughan Williams, The Oxford Book
of Carols, (London, 1928), and the good abridg-
ment by his associate Elizabeth Poston, The
Penguin Book of Christmas Carols, (London,
1965). See Adams' Dancing Christmas Carols
($6.95 from the Sharing Company) for some 30
dances to Christmas Carols.

to adjust our ways to the ways of others if
community is not to be torn completely apart is
learned through this exercise. People in groups
of six or eight are tied together around the
waists with rolls of crepe paper. The group is
then to move without breaking the crepe paper
and without talking. People thus need to be
highly sensitive to the directions in which
others wish to go and be responsive to others'
movements. One cannot have ones own way all the
time but must adjust ones movements somewhat to
those in the group; or if one chooses, a person
may break off from the group with the subsequent
loss of tension and intention.

COMMUNAL DANCING AND EQUALITY

That dance effects a sense of equality among the
participants can be seen from two phenomena:
1) the use of dance in initiatory rites and
other rites emphasising the equality of all, and
2) the restrictions barring social unequals from
dancing together in church and the eventual prohibition of communal dancing in church. We will
review these phenomena and then explore ways to
dance today to include all in a sense of
equality.

Initiation into new communities often included

dancing with others in the communities to symbolize and effect equality of all. The practice
of the new priest circling the altar with his
new brethren was eventually eliminated in the
Catholic Church [51] but persists even today in
the Orthodox Church ordination. [52] Similarly
up until 1700 in Germany, the faculty performed
ring dances with the students when bestowing
the Ph.D. [53]

The use of dance to emphasize the equality of
all is seen principally in the dance Macabre of
the middle ages. Macabre comes from the Arabic
makabr meaning church yards. [54] There was an
early church practice associated with belief
in resurrection which we will explore in the
chapter on rejoicing. But the festivals around
death in the Middle Ages emphasize the final
death of all and hence equality of all. That
dance was used so centrally in this festival

---

51. Backman, op. cit., p. 91.

52. Zernov, Orthodox Encounter, op. cit., pp.
84-85. A similar dance is used in the marriage
rite and in the Serbian rite of brotherhood.

53. Gerhardus van der Leeuw, op. cit., p. 32.

54. Walter Sorell, Dance Through the Ages, (New
York, 1967), p. 30.

testifies to the equalizing effect of dancing.[55]

The equalizing effects of dance were expressly
cultivated by bishops in France (particularly
Rheims) where they lowered themselves to dance
with subordinates in a game involving the passing of a ball to emphasize the basic equality of
all. [56] But this practice in December and
similar ones which evolved in the Festival of
Fools in January were too revolutionary to be
long tolerated by an increasingly authoritarian
and hierarchial church.

THE RESTRICTION AND PROHIBITION OF COMMUNAL DANCING

At first the church authorities attempted to
minimize the revolutionary effect of dance by
restricting people to dancing with their social
equals. In Paris choir boys danced on Innocents'
Day, the sub-deacons on Epiphany, the deacons on
St. Stephen's Day, and the priests on St. John's
Day. [57] But these restrictions were difficult

---

55. For a fuller description of the Dance of
Death see Backman, op. cit., pp. 131-154.

56. Ibid., p. 50.

57. Ibid., p. 51.

to enforce as dancing was so often infectious.
Harvey Cox has analyzed the revolutionary effect
of dancing and the Festival of Fools in guiding
people to see all social structures as less than
absolute. Even the Bible was mocked in this
general effort to let God be God. [58]

The Catholic church effort to prohibit corporate
dancing from the church and graveyards and to
prohibit Christians from dancing with others
even outside the church extends throughout per-
iods of church crisis from Augustine through the
eighteenth century. This history has been well
recounted elsewhere. [59] Our concern is to see
the dynamics of corporate dancing revealed by
such prohibitions. The prohibitions were designed to keep Christians from intimate contact
with Christians of other social classes and from
intimate contact with those outside the Christian
community. After reviewing some cases of this
prohibition, we will develop ways of dancing in
Christian worship to foster this very idea of
equality.

---

58. Harvey Cox, The Feast of Fools, (New York,
1969), passim.
59. See Backman, op. cit., pp. 154-161.

We have already referred to the prohibition of
communal dance within the church itself in
connection with the Festival of Fools. These
prohibitions began in the seventh century but
were not totally successful until the seventeenth century. [60] Antecedent to these prohibitions, prohibitions had been made against
dancing with non-Christians. Isidore (A.D. 560-
639), bishop of Seville, propagated such prohibitions for such dancing condoned the worth
of the pagan with whom one danced and led to
further association with pagans. [61] Later
prohibitions by Christian and Jewish hierarchy
alike testify to the power of dancing to develop
a sense of comradery and equality among Jews and
Christians. [62]

---

60. Ibid., A similar pattern of restrictions on
dance for similar reasons was imposed on revival
meetings in the South. In the 19th century revival meetings although blacks and whites were
seated separately, they all joined together in
moving to the marching out hymn. The practice
was eliminated because of the equalizing effects.
Cf. Charles Johnson, The Frontier Camp Meeting,
pp. 41ff.
61. Ibid., p. 35. Also in Judaism, Rabbis had
long held that dancing with others honored them
and uplifted their worth. Thus rabbis regularly
danced with the bride before or during the wedding
as we will later note.
62. Cecil Roth, The Jews in the Renaissance,(Philadelphia, 1964), especially pp. 275ff. The presence of dancing in so many ecumenical worship
services today testifies again to the dancing-
equalizing dynamic.

50

COMMUNAL DANCING FOR EQUALITY IN THE CHURCH TODAY

For standard Sunday morning worship services,
the minister himself by his movement may help
effect a sense of equality. The architecture
of the church is also important to emphasize this
equality. The position of the minister in a
pulpit raised above the people is hardly the
symbol to emphasize the equality of all. For a
minister to preach about the equality of all
and the community   of all while perched high
above the people in the pulpit foster something
other than a sense of equality. In the final
chapter of this book, we will explore more
extensively the demonic dimensions of the min -
ister in the pulpit. Here let it suffice to say
that Jesus and his followers for three hundred
years gave their sermons while seated (e.g. Luke
4.20). Chrysostom was the first to preach from a
lectern and did so because of his weak voice (the
lectern was positioned so people could be around
it.) [63] Let the minister give the sermon and
witness from the communion table on a level with
the people or while moving among the people so
that the people look not just to the minister or
back wall but to one another. Thus the people will

---

63. Massey Shepherd, Jr. Class notes, Spring 1968.

see again that coming to God is coming toward
each other. [64] People in the congregation may
at first feel uncomfortable to have the minister
on their level or so close to them; but let the
minister point out that Christ purposely makes
us feel uncomfortable in this way as he did
with Peter (John 13.6-8) and so makes us realize
that we are important and must respond.

For more informal services, the blind trust walk
will help children feel they have an equally
important role to play. In the blind walk each
person joins one other person. Then one person
in each pair closes both eyes and is led by the
other person, who holds both hands. After walking around for some time, the two change roles:
the one who has been leading closes both eyes
and the one who has been led opens both eyes and
does the leading for a time. Some middle aged
persons have trouble trusting very far (in fact
some are not able to take even a step in this
fashion). One could well have a minute of this
exercise as the opening confession for the worship service. Then after discussing the reasons
we can trust others because Christ is in each

---

64. For new patterns of church architecture see
Frederic Debuyst, Modern Architecture and Christian Celebration, (Richmond, 1968).

52

one, we could return to the trust walk for a
longer period of time. If a person is at first
unable to walk while the eyes are closed, one may
be able to allow one's hands to be led in motion
while one remains seated. After allowing the
hands to be led for a time, then one may feel
free to respond with the whole body. Some
people may be initially afraid of these experiences or may be too self-critical because of
their experience. Evaluative time at the end of
the service should be planned to allow expression
of the people's fears and failures as well as
successes so that people will realize that they
are not alone in their reactions. Other T group
exercises may be adapted in this way where they
may incarnate the ideas of Christian training. [65]

Almost any dancing in church in which the minister participates with the people on an equal
footing has an equalizing effect. Children feel
especially included as equals in dancing, for
dancing is something they can do; whereas much
of the worship service is verbal and intellectual
and over their heads. In our less formal service
at Arlington Community Church, we pushed back

---

65. The guide to "T" group techniques and centers
is William C. Shutz's Joy: Expanding Human
Awareness, (New York, 1967).

the pews and put down rugs in the front of the
nave so that people could sit on the floor, sit
in the pews, stand, or move as they wished.
The way was thus cleared for dancing during any
song by which people were moved. People often
moved in small circles of four or five on the
choruses of songs and sometimes joined together
so that nearly everyone moved more slowly in one
large circle. On occasion we developed several
concentric circles. The smaller children were
in the inner circles with others who wished to
move more rapidly while most older people walked
more slowly in the outer circles.

COMMUNAL DANCING AND DIVERSITY

It is important to allow a diversity of participation in dance from sitting in the pews to
very swift moving. When we truly understand our
interrelation in community, we will understand
what dancers mean when they say that those also
dance who simply sit and watch. It is important
to avoid a tyranny of dance which may turn some
against dance. Augustine apparently experienced
such a tyranny which influenced his attitude
toward dance: "Those who have not danced are
blamed, reproached, accused, banished." [66]

---

66. Augustine, "Speech 311," Migne, P.L., op.cit,
38, col. 1415,Eng. trans. Backman, op.cit.,p. 33.

54

Some may say that a community encouraging true
diversity would not dictate a choreography to
others. Of course we are aiming toward an undictated diversity within community; but adults
especially need to learn how to move their bodies
in worship. It is our experience that once
people have been led to discover how their
bodies can move, they begin to move on their own.
A scene of such diverse movement may seem
chaotic to those who have a view of community
as conformity. (Western Christianity still too
often proposes uniformity as the expression of
community: "There should be uniform attitude
of body kept by all participants, for this is a
sign of the community and unity of the assembly."
[67] But diverse movement and activity by participants in worship is true to the most Orthodox
Christian worship. The people's activity in
Eastern Orthodox worship is like jazz improvi-
zation with bows, prostrations, and signs of the
cross undictated by the priest or any pre-
arranged pattern of bells. Thus some will feel
moved to stand while others kneel and still
others prostrate themselves [68] Such a scene
in worship affirms the diversity of action in

67. Rev. Wm. Carr, trans., General Instructions
of the Roman Missal,(Quincy, Ill.,1969), pp.6-7.
68. Nicholas Zernov, Eastern Christendom, (London,
1961), p. 238.

life in the world; and such a scene in worship
encourages the people to think of the hoped for
kingdom of God on earth as one embracing plural-
ities and not just uniformities. Development
of this scene in an innovative worship service
comes with time and communal experience. After
six months' experience of dance in innovative
worship at Arlington Community Church, the
congregation often began dancing spontaneously.

Several simple choreographies which stress this
need for allowing diversity may be the first
step toward freeing the people to develop diversity of actions in corporate worship.
Margaret Taylor has taught us a simple pattern
of living sculpture within which people respond
to the song "Amen." [69]

Margaret invites the people (as many as wish to
participate) to assemble in groups of five in
the aisles and in the chancel of the church. The
people number off one through five within each
group. Then, as the choir or all sing a five
fold amen, each person takes and holds a position
which expresses for him or her the word, scripture,

---

69. Margaret Taylor led workshops and worship in
dance at Pacific School of Religion in 1968 and
1977.

56

emotion, hymn, or work of art being considered.
(Number one takes a position as the first amen
is sung, number two takes a position as the
second amen is sung, and so forth.) While
numbers one through three may be encouraged to
strike poses quite independently from one
another, numbers four and five could be asked to
position themselves to make a whole out of the
group. At the end of the sequence, all should
remain frozen in position so that those in other
groups may view the sculpture. (Some may wish
to move around these living sculptures to view
them from many different angles.) Each doing
of this sequence takes only a minute or two;
then the group may be dissolved, renumbered, and
instructed to create another sculpture expressing another aspect of the text, art work, or
hymn. (There are as many different sculptures
possible as there are words or passages in the
Bible, or hymns in the hymn book, or slides of
great art works in a local library.)

For example, in the first formation, each person
could be asked to take a position that expresses
a different word for an emotion Abraham must
have felt when he was called upon to sacrifice
his son; in a second time through the sequence,
all could be asked to take positions expressing
words for the emotion Isaac felt when he realized

his father's intentions and that God had asked
his father to do it; and in a third time through
the sequence, the people might express how
Abraham and/or Isaac felt when God announced
that Isaac was to be shared. Most important, the
leader should allow each person a few moments
(before each formation is created) to think of
the emotion he or she would feel as Abraham or
Isaac and the word that expresses that emotion.
And after the formations have been created, the
leaders should move among the creations and ask
each person to say aloud the one word for the
emotion which they are expressing by their
stance.

In the foregoing choreography individual freedom
and diversity is allowed but all within contin-
uing concern for the shape of the total community. [70] Another choreography which allows this
same diversity but within an obvious context of

------

70. Dance choir members could be present to see
how the congregation's members move and later
form these movements into a dance to be performed
that evening or at a later worship service a
week or two later. (Slides of those congregation's sculptures could be taken and pro-
jected as a backdrop to the dance choir's
presentation in a later worship service.)

community ismovement to Johnny Mathis' song "I
Heard the Forest Praying." The lyrics of the
song speak of the many purposes for which for-
ests serve (a playground for children, a pro-
tection for lovers etc. : purposes for which
the church also has a calling.) Have the people
form a large circle. (If there are many people,
have them form several concentric circles.) If
the people must remain in pews, have all face
the center aisle. In the center of the circles
or in the aisle have one or two or more dancers
interpret the different scenes of the song while
the people in the circles or in the pews hold
hands and raise arms up in the position of
prayer earlier prescribed by Paul. The people
are the forest and can sway their arms as
branches and respond to the dancers by reaching
out to cover or comfort them. The soloist,
Thelma Bachelor, who did the solo part in the
midst of a circle of several hundred people reported that she had never felt so moved in interaction with so many others. Some said that now
they knew what community could and should become!

CHAPTER III

DANCING AND REPENTANCE

Dancing in the Judeo-Christian tradition has
been associated with the experiences that life
is not determined by the past or old self.
Bondage to the past may be shaken off by dancing
to free attention to feel new intentions. Let
us study this freeing dynamic of dancing in the
Judeo-Christian traditions, then explore the
psychology and theology of this dynamic and
finally explore ways of congregational movement
for our time to experience this freedom and new
intention.

OLD TESTAMENT AND JEWISH EVIDENCE

In the Old Testament and subsequent Jewish traditions, dance celebrates and effects the end of
slavery to the past and the beginning of new
freedom to act in the world and create new
community. This dynamic is present in the
Biblical account of the first dance (at the
Exodus), the Jewish commentaries on that account,
and the Hassidic explanation for the Jews learn-
ing to dance. After exploring the foregoing

59

60

we will examine the prophets' practice of dance
to achieve these same effects.

At the Exodus (Exodus 15.20), Miriam led the
women in dance to celebrate the overthrow of the
Egyptians and the end of Israelite slavery. In
a discussion of this dancing and singing in the
late Beshallach Midrash, the following observa-
tion is made:

> In the Messianic Age, there will no longer
> be any troubles, for it says, 'Because the
> former troubles are forgotten (Isa. LXV.
> 16)', and they shall obtain gladness and
> joy. (ib.xxxv.10)   71

Thus, dance is linked to a forgetting of and
freeing from the troubling past. Of course the
foregoing does not prove that the early Israe-
lites had such a sophisticated understanding of
the effects of dance; but the dance at the Exodus
is most appropriate as a watershed between
slavery and freedom, the past and the future.

The founder of Hassidism, Israel Baal Shem Tov,
saw this same dynamic of dance in telling the
story of why he learned to dance and set off

---

71. "Beshallach," (Exodus), XXIII. 11, The
Midrash, op. cit., p. 290.

the great religious revival in Eastern European
Judaism in the Eighteenth century. He learned
to dance to aid a jailed Jew gain his freedom.
If one could dance well, he would be freed from
bondage. Here again we have the association of
dancing and people being freed to act. [72]

Prophets (nabi) used dance to effect the loss of
preoccupation with self and past concerns. This
dynamic is revealed most clearly in Saul's con-
tacts with the prophetic bands. Saul's first
contact with the prophets (I Samuel 10, 5ff.)
will be examined in the final chapter of this
paper to see the role of dance in increasing
intention. In this chapter we will examine
Saul's last contact with such a group (I Samuel
19.18ff). In this account the loss of self-
consciousness in dancing is obvious in the
uninhibited nakedness of Saul and the others.
The loss of preoccupation with the past concerns

---

72. Louis I. Newman, The Hasidic Anthology, (New
York, 1934), p. 66. This dynamic is further
emphasized in the American experience by the fact
that dance in black worship was prohibited by
white legislatures because such dancing resulted
in blacks feeling too strong a sense of freedom.
(c.f. Lynne Fauley Emery, "Sacred Dance," Black
Dance In the United States From 1619 to 1970,
pp. 119-138.)

is obvious in the actions of Saul's messengers
and finally Saul himself who came to the prophets
with the purpose of taking David but became caught
up in the spirit of prophesying (dancing) and
forgot their former concern. [73]

Chapter four (which discusses the Israelite
rejection of mournful dancing and development
of rejoiceful dancing) will provide further
evidence that the form of Israelite dancing
asserts a people's responsibility for the world
and their ability to effect change in the world.

EVIDENCE IN CRITICAL LITERATURE

Christian literature testifies to a similar use
of dance to effect people's freedom to act in
the world. Early Christian writings and later
hymnody evidence the use of dance to shake off
bondage to the devil and disease. Later literature influenced by Christian ideas developed
the picture of the devil and those in bondage to
the devil as unmoving. We will explore first
this early use of dance and then the literary

---

73. That prophesying implies dancing in this
context and for further information on dancing
among the prophets, see Alfred Haldar, Associations of Cult Prophets Among the Ancient Semites,
(Uppsala, 1945), passim.

understanding of non-movement -- an understanding
which will create a framework for our own subsequent discussion of philosophy and theology
of dancing as repentance.

Gregory of Nazianzus, the bishop of Constantinople
(whose position within Eastern Orthodoxy and
attitude toward dance we have already discussed),
associates the following: "May we flee from all
the chains of the devil" in performing "triumphant ring dances." [74] In another address,
Gregory urges the people to attend ceremonies
using dances at the graves of martyrs "for the
manifest casting out of devils, the prevention
of sickness and the knowledge of things to
come." [75] A church hymn sung and danced on
Easter in the twelfth century echoes this same
dynamic:

> Zion, rejoice, dance the ring dance:
> Sing for our brethren!
> Stamp the feet, clap the hands,
> No restraint in gesture!
> Thy David strikes the tambourine,

---

74. Gregory of Nazianzus, "Speech II to Gregory
of Nyssa," Migne, P.Gr., op. cit., Vol. 35, Col.
838, Eng. trans., Backman, op. cit., p. 31.

75. Gregory of Nazianzus, "Speech 24," Ibid.,
co. 1191, Eng. trans., Backman, op. cit., p. 42.

64

He turns unto the dead.
Thus is exorcised the king
of the underworld.   76

Another medieval hymn sings of dancing and
"trampling vices under foot." [77] These are
only fragments; but the following records reveal
the commonness within the early church of the
use of dance to shake off the devil, disease,
and all that enslaves people and holds them down.

The Therapeutae (a Jewish sect that may have
converted to Early Christianity) did a dance (in
imitation of Miriam's) which may have had the
effect of curing disease. [78] Whether or not
this group was ever Christian, their practice

---

76. From Analecta Hymna 21, 37, Eng. trans.,
Backman, op. cit., p. 46.

77. From Analecta Hymna 1, 137, Eng. trans.,
Backman, op. cit., p. 45.

78. F.H. Colson, trans., "The Contemplative Life,"
Philo, (Cambridge, 1954), IX, pp. 104-169. See
especially pp. 165-167. Also see Fred C. Conybeare, op. cit., This latter volume sets forth
the Greek, Latin, and Armenian texts of Philo's
work and the Greek and Latin versions of Eusebius'
commentary and gives a conclusive defense of the
authorship by Philo. Of course the Therapeutae
and their dancing rituals were dedicated to worship; but that these rituals and the very name of
the group itself were connected with curing bodies
as well as souls from disease, is suggested by
Philo himself: Colson, DVC 2.

was common among Christians as the church his-
torian Eusebius (A.D. 260-340), Bishop of
Caesarea, testifies in calling the Therapeutae
practice Christian and a practice "it is still
our custom to the present day to perform." [79]

There has been a long association between dancing
and healing in Christianity. Often great leaders
of dance in the church have been noted for their
healing. Gregory the Wonder Worker (A.D. 213-
270), Bishop of Pontus, who devised special
dances on festivals for martyrs, is just one
example. [80] The use of dance in treating mental
disease is an area of renewed interest in our
time. [81]

---

80. Backman, op. cit., p. 22. The full title of
Backman's book and much of its evidence points
to this same connection: Religious Dances in the
Christian Church and Popular Medicine.

81. The literature is too vast to be recounted
here. A good, although incomplete, survey of
theses done in the field is published by the American Assoc. for Health, Physical Education, and
Recreation and is titled Bibliographies of Dance
Research. A graphic exposition of use of dance
"for unlocking the personalities and capabilities
of retarded children" is Norma Canner's book And
A Time to Dance, (Boston, 1968). Norma Canner
is a dancer who works with the Massachusetts
Department of Mental Health.

Much literature influenced by Christian ideas
came to associate ills with non-movement and to
see the devil and those in demonic bondage as
non-moving and antagonistic to dance. Dante
Alighieri's Divine Comedy depicts the Devil
as one encased in a cake of ice, unable to move
except as the devil "stood forth at mid-breast
from the ice." [82] (How like most ministers in
pulpits)

In Dante's vision, the closer one comes to God
the more active one becomes: the angels dance
around the Lord. (In the final chapter of this
paper, we will explore further the dimension of
God and God's followers as ones who move.) In
accordance with the foregoing scheme, William
Shakespeare's characters expose themselves by
their attitudes toward dance and music. For
instance, Capulet says to his cousin what is
painfully obvious in their attitude toward love
and others: "you and I are past our dancing
days." (Romeo and Juliet, I, v, 32). [83] And
Shylock's reaction to dancing is what one would

82. John Sinclair, trans., The Divine Comedy of
Dante Alighieri, Inferno, Canto 34, (New York,
1961), p. 421.
83. G. G. Harrison, ed., Shakespeare, Major Plays,
(New York, 1948), p. 240.

expect from such a villian. He bids Jessica:

> Lock up my doors, and when you hear the
> drum
> And vile squealing of the wry-necked fife,
> Clambor not you up to the casements then,
> Nor thrust your head into the public street
> To gaze on Christian fools with varnished
> faces,
> But stop my house's ears, I mean my
> casements.
> Let not the sound of shallow foppery enter
> my sober house.   84
> (Merchant of Venice, II, v, 29-36).

How many are unfortunately like Shylock in their
attitudes toward dance in worship and would cut
the heart out of life! Similar literary insights
into the correlation of dancing with character
are collected by Gerhardus van der Leeuw. [85]

THE PSYCHOLOGY AND THEOLOGY OF REPENTANCE

Repentance means a change of mind -- a turning
around and a going in a different direction.
Repentance is a shift of attention which brings
with it a new intention. Repentance means a
shift away from attention to oneself (flesh) to
attention toward God (the Spirit) -- a shift
from fixation or non-movement to movement.

---

84. Ibid., p. 313.
85. Gerhardus van der Leeuw, op. cit., passim.

First we will examine the orientations suggested
by the terms "flesh" and "spirit" and then
explore how dancing aids a shift from one
orientation of attention to the other.

When the New Testament writers speak of flesh
and spirit ($\sigma\acute{\alpha}\rho\xi$ and $\pi\nu\epsilon\hat{\upsilon}\mu\alpha$) they use
these words in an entirely different way than
that to which we are accustomed today. The
biblical use of these terms "is not to be understood in terms of form and substance." [86] The
uses of these words "represent the whole man
under different aspects" [87] and so stand in
strong contrast to the Greek or Cartesian anti-
theses of spirit and flesh or mind and body. [88]
as J.A.T. Robinson spells out in his definitive
work, The Body:

> For Paul, while $\pi\nu\epsilon\hat{\upsilon}\mu\alpha$, spirit, when
> it is used of man, is that in virtue of
> which he is open to and transmits the life
> of God . . ., $\sigma\acute{\alpha}\rho\xi$ is man in contrast
> with God. [89]

---

86. John A. T. Robinson, The Body: A Study in
Pauline Theology, (London, 1963), p. 17.

87. Ibid., p. 13.

88. Ibid., p. 23.

89. Ibid., p. 19.

It is helpful to consider Paul's statement in
Romans 8.6:

> To set the mind on the flesh is death, but
> to set the mind on the Spirit is life and
> peace.

To focus my attention on myself and so orient
myself around myself leads to death. To focus
attention on God and to remain open to God's
impulse (and so orient myself as an instrument
of God) leads to life.

The role of attention becomes clearer in psychologically considering its role in using any
instrument in one's effort to function in the
world. For instance, if in using a hammer, one
focuses on the handle of the hammer or focuses
on one's own hand instead of the hammer's head,
then the hammer no longer functions as an
instrumental extension of the body. Similarly,

> If a pianist shifts his attention from the
> piece he is playing to the observation of
> what he is doing with his fingers while
> playing it, he gets confused and may have
> to stop. This happens generally if we
> switch our focal attention to particulars
> of which we had previously been aware only
> in their subsidiary role.
> The kind of clumsiness which is due to the
> fact that focal attention is directed to
> the subsidiary element of an action is

70

commonly known as self-consciousness.   90

To function effectively in the world, one must
first overcome fixation of one's self: self-
consciousness, psychologically; self-centeredness,
sociologically; and flesh, theologically.

Thus Paul is not attacking the body when he
attacks "the flesh", but rather Paul is attacking
a particular orientation to one's own body and
one's own life -- an orientation marked by
preoccupation with self and fixation on one's
problems,   91 because in this orientation of
flesh one attempts to run one's own life, seeks
to solve one's own problems in isolation from

---

90. Michael Polanyi, Personal Knowledge: Towards
a Post-Critical Philosophy, (New York, 1964),
p. 56.
91. It is crucial that we see that Paul's theology is not the attack on the material body that
many preachers have represented it to be. Unfortunately many dancers have traced the church
objection to dance to Paul and not to the
preachers' Greek or Cartesian misinterpretation
of Paul's writings. This has damaged the cause
of dance in the church not only by classing a
major authority of the church as opposed to dance
but also in leading dancers to avoid or attack
Paul's writings. (See for example Walter
Sorell's The Dance Through the Ages, (New York,
1967), p. 38. In reality Paul's writings are
a fund of arguments and texts for dance in worship
Romans 12.1, I Corinthians 6.19-20, and others
cited by Robinson, op. cit., passim.

others' lives, but only succeeds in further
fixation.

Dancing is a practice of the <u>via negativa</u> and
as such aids repentance (the shift of attention
away from self concern and its resultant preoccupation with the past and present problems of
self). <u>Via negativa</u> is the negative way which
entails the elimination of all thoughts which
grasp the mind. Vladimir Lossky, the leading
Orthodox theologian of this century, wrote that
practices of the <u>via negativa</u> lead to repentance
and are in themselves repentance. [92] Body
movement is for the purpose of aiding this
shift of attention. [93]

Engagement in any activity could bring about a
shift of attention from that which was depressing
one; but body movement shifts the attention away
from prior thoughts without filling the mind
with other thoughts concerning the particulars
of the new activity; for "dance is the art of
which we are the stuff," [94] with no external

---

92. Vladimir Lossky, <u>The Mystical Theology of
the Eastern Church</u>, (London, 1957), p. 238.

93. <u>Ibid.</u>, p. 210.

94. Havelock Ellis, <u>The Dance of Life</u>, (New York,
1923), p. 62.

instruments necessary. Thus in dance the mind
is freed to be drawn to new thoughts and new
intentions. To further understand this dynamic
of dance, I had met with Michael Polanyi, for he
had written extensively on the structure of
extending one's in-dwelling as a mind-body-in-
world and had noted that the <u>via negativa</u> is the
way all must act if they are to come into
relationship with any reality of which they were
previously unaware. [95] After discussing this
dynamic with Polanyi in Berkeley, I experienced
the following which I later related to him:

> Walking back from our meeting, I had occa-
> sion to stop in an art gallery. The way
> some people move around in front of a
> painting there is most instructive. They
> literally dance around deploying themselves
> in all sorts of ways until they begin to
> move in new ways and you know they have
> been grasped!
> In that positioning they feel the intensity,
> the intention of the work of art and the
> world. Of course, many others preoccupied
> with their own thoughts walk by and never
> position themselves in ways to feel any-
> thing. Let us hope that more will take
> time to dance. [96]

In the foregoing description we have moved beyond
the freeing dynamic of dance (the turning away

95. Polanyi, op. cit., pp. 195-202.
96. Adams to Polanyi, personal correspondence,
January 12, 1968.

from the fixation on self: the flesh) to
attention to God and the new intention that
results: the spirit. As Gerhardus van der
Leeuw has observed, the dance not only unchains,
but it chains as well. [97] Dancing frees the
mind; but for what? Dancing frees the mind for
the strongest reality to grasp. It is our faith
that that strongest reality is God. The increase
in this new intention is the subject of the
final chapter.

With the foregoing framework in mind, let us
look at one experience of repentance through
dance and then try to understand why this experience occurred. Working in both the Pacific
School of Religion Dance Choir and Newman Hall's
University Arts' Council in Bekeley, I had
arranged a Saturday evening worship in motion
with congregational participation for Newman
Hall. I had not realized that every Saturday
evening was a major time for the hearing of
confessions; and the confessions were heard in
booths at the rear of the nave in which we were
holding our worship in motion. During that
Saturday evening, over forty people entered the

---

97. van der Leeuw, op. cit., p. 21.

74

sanctuary with the drawn faces of those disturbed
and about to confess. Seeing the worship in
motion in process, almost all of these people
who had come to confess joined the worship.
Half way through the evening of dancing, the
priest had given up hope of any of his people
coming to confession and stood at the back of
the sanctuary watching the worship. By the end
of the evening, people (who were dancing instead
of sitting in the confessional were going away
from the church saying that they no longer felt
the need for confession. [98]

Let us understand this change or shift of intention by reference to the framework of flesh and
spirit. The people had come attending to their
problems and weighted down by such attention.
By dancing the people forgot these past problems.
Those who believe that one should face one's
problems and solve them oneself will no doubt
abhor such a solution; but dancing is a practice

---

98. This occurrence is reminiscent of an association between dancing and clean conscience in a
eucharistic prayer of a Gallican sacramentary in
the 7th century: "We beseech thee, almighty Father,
eternal God, deliver us from all temptation, give
us help in every conflict. . . . Grant that we
may worship thee with a pure heart; let us serve
thee with all our strength." Evelyn Underhill,
Eucharistic Prayers From Ancient Liturgies,
(London, 1939), p. 55.

which would have us solve problems by moving ahead to a new orientation in life attending to God and others and not just ourselves. Of course such dancing does not solve the particular problems that persist in a particular life; but dancing raises one to a new relationship in which one is better able to deal with the problems.

DANCING FOR REPENTANCE IN THE CHURCH TODAY

In Chapter One, we suggested several ways for congregations to move and help effect the self-sacrifice of repentance today. Movements to Romans 12.1 and the hymn "Into Your Hands" were outlined to help bring people to an openness to hear the gospel. Standing during the reading of the gospel was suggested as a way to increase the attention to the good news. In what remains of this chapter let us explore other ways to aid repentance and/or reinforce such repentance.

The second stanza of "God of Grace and God of Glory" sums up much of what we have detailed as the dynamic of repentance:

> Lo! the hosts of evil round us,
> Scorn thy Christ, assail his ways
> From the fears that long have bound us,
> Free our hearts to faith and praise.
> Grant us wisdom, grant us courage,

> For the living of these days,
> For the living of these days.   99

Margaret Taylor has suggested a simple movement
in which all may participate to heighten the
meaning of this hymn while singing either stanza
two or one. [100]

The movement is one of literal turning which is
most appropriate for repentance. While singing
most of the stanza, all face the chancel area
(the cross or communion table) and as many as
possible move forward to these areas to offer
themselves for the purposes of freeing and re-
strengthening mentioned in the hymn. But after
singing "Grant us wisdom, grant us courage,"
all turn around and face the opposite direction
(the doors to the world) while singing "for the
living of these days" in the second stanza, or
"for the facing of this hour" in the first
stanza. This movement could be done at the time
of offering as repentance or at the recessional
as a reinforcement of earlier repentance. If
it is done as the recessional, then after the
turning all could continue singing the hymn

---

99. Harry Emerson Fosdick, "God of Grace and God
of Glory," Pilgrim Hymnal, (Boston, 1964), p. 366.
100.Margaret Taylor at workshops and worship in
dancing at Pacific School of Religion.

and recess out of the nave into the world. (In
either event, having hymn books in hand obviously
detracts from the freeing impact of this movement; so it is best to rehearse either stanza
one or two with the people so they know it by
heart before adding the movement.)

This literal turning may be used as a congregational response to numerous Biblical passages
on repentance and to prayers and hymns which
suggest a turning. Even though people remain
standing in pews, they can turn to face in many
different directions. The congregation could be
led to read prayers of confession while facing
the back of the church (symbolizing the life
from which they have come and to which they are
bound); then all could turn toward the front of
the church in response to receiving the word of
assurance.

Later having been restrengthened by communion
the congregation could be led to turn their
attention back toward their lives (turning
toward the back of the church) while reading the
prayer of dedication and singing the recessional
hymn. At Arlington Commnity Church, as a
response to the good news we have often made a
new entrance into the nave (going out to assemble
in an adjacent room or hall and then reentering

the nave together singing a lively hymn). This
movement helps shake off the past and the
thoughts which come from sitting and brooding
about the past and so frees us for the new to
which the gospel calls us.

Other simple physical acts can aid this turning
away from the way of flesh: the devilish way
in which we are chained by our insistence on
clinging to and directing every detail of our
own lives. Sister Tina Bernal has devised movements for "Stick of Bamboo" that would lead us
to a less grasping, less striving, less clutching
approach to our actions and lives. [100] The
lyrics for the song are as follows:

> You take a stick of bamboo
> You take a stick of bamboo
> You take a stick of bamboo,
> And you put it in the water
> Hosanna
> > Chorus: River, river she come down
> > River, river she come down.

Some people may be invited to kneel in rows with
the minister in the chancel or nave and those
remaining in the pews may imitate the movements
with their arms. During the repetition of

---

101. Sister Tina Bernal in workshops of dance in
worship at Newman Hall, Berkeley, California.

"You take a stick of bamboo," each person should
imagine that their whole life with all its
action and trouble is like a stick of bamboo in
a vertical position in front of them. On the
first "take", one should grasp the stick with
one's left hand; on the second "take," one should
grasp the stick with one's right hand just above
one's left hand; and on the third "take," one
should move one's left hand above one's right
hand to a new position of grasping. This closed
fisted holding to the stick and to our lives is
typical of the way of the flesh. Then on "and
you put it in the water," one should place the
imaginary stick in a low horizontal position in
the imaginary river in front of one and let it
go! (The river may represent God; and thus we
let go of our lives and past actions entrusting
them to God's care.) The "Hosanna" should be
accompanied by a lifting and a bending backwards
of the hands, arms, and head -- offering oneself
to God and opening oneself for salvation. Then
the chorus ("River, river she come down") may
be accompanied by movement of the hands vertically
down and then horizontally to the right to symbolize the rain and river carrying the stick
away. (This cleansing act by God may also be
seen as the new experience of grace in which our
acts are carried out not independently but with
dependence and interdependence.) The inter-

dependence of all can be emphasized by the second stanza of the song which repeats "We travel on the river." This lyric, which continues to emphasize our dependence on God's grace (the river) can emphasize our interrelation with others by having all move their arms in a simple paddling or rowing action. This is a particularly appropriate action in the nave; for the designation of the place of worship as "nave" comes from "navis" which means ship and is to remind us that we are to pull together to reach the goal of God's kingdom on earth.

Carlton Whitlach, pastor of the United Church of Christ in Moraga, California, has developed a movement in which he as minister gathers up the cares of his people and offers them to God. He simply moves down the nave with his hands cupped before him and says to his people, "Give me your cares and troubled thoughts." He brings his opened hands close to people and encourages them to move their own hands toward his as symbolic of placing or throwing their cares into his hands. After gathering up the cares in this way, he takes them to the altar table and deposits them there. Many people have reported a great sense of release through Carlton

Whitlach's practice. 103

Another sequence helps the people leave behind
the past and open to a new future. During the
offertory, those who wish could come forward to
place their offering on the altar and so help
all see that we offer ourselves and not just
money in the act of worship. Those who come
forward could remain in the front of the church
and form concentric circles around the altar for
the doxology. As all sing the doxology, those
in the circles join hands, face into the circle,
and move as follows: on the words "Praise God
from whom all blessings flow," the people take
four steps forward into the circle while raising
up each others' hands above their heads; on the
words "Praise God all creatures here below,"
the people take four steps backwards while
bowing from the waist deeply and lowering to
their sides the hands which remain joined to
others; then on the words, "Praise God above the

103. Similar effects have been felt by those
moving to one section of Margit Werres' choreography for the Lord's Prayer: the movement to
"Forgive us our trespasses as we forgive those
who trespass against us." I have incorporated
this movement into my own chorography for the
Lord's Prayer to be found in appendix two.
Margit was a master student of Mary Wigman.

heavenly host," all move as they did to the
first phrase; and on the words, "Praise to God,
Son, and Holy Ghost," they repeat the movements
to the second phrase. Finally, on the "Amen,"
all straighten up and raise their joined hands
above their heads.

CHAPTER IV

DANCING AND REJOICING

The Jewish and Christian use of dance to create
community and to shake off bondage (experiences
which we explored in chapters two and three)
naturally led to the association of rejoicing
with dancing. The development of the rejoicing
kind of dance in Jewish and Christian worship
has accompanied a recognition that people have
the possibility and responsibility to change the
conditions in the world and that the material
world (including people s' bodies) is good and for
people's use. We will study this development,
see how it springs from a view of the world as
potentially good and in our charge, and then
explore practical ways in which we may use the
rejoicing kinds of dancing in worship to bring
about a consciousness in our people of the good-
ness of their bodies and their possibilities and
responsibilities in the material world.

JEWISH REJOICEFUL DANCE AND
RECOGNITION OF POSSIBILITY

First let us see how the development of the rejoiceful Israelite dance emphasized the Israelite's recognition of their own responsibility

for the world rather than the subjugation of
their welfare and the world to the cyclical
dying and rising of God. In this development
let us note that the declines and reemergences
of the rejoiceful dance in worship appear to
vary directly with the declines and reemergences
of the people's belief in their ability to affect
the world around them.

The recognition of people's responsibility and
possibility to change the material world is
evident in the Israelite rejection of the mournful dance of the Semitic milieu (a dance which
emphasized God's responsibility for the world
and the future) and the Israelite's accompanying
acceptance of a rejoiceful dance which emphasized
people's responsibility. The mournful dance to
God (pesach: leaping or limping) performed by
the priests of Baal in I Kings 18.28 was based
on a belief that the world's problems were
traceable to the God being dead and that the
future of the world depended on the God rising
which the dancing might evoke. Thus in the
Syriac, the principle word for dance in different
conjugations meant dancing and mourning. [104]

104. William Robertson Smith, Lectures on the Re-
ligion of the Semites, (London, 1914), p. 432.
Haldar, op. cit., p. 60ff. Julian Morgenstern.
"The Etymological History of Three Hebrew Syno-
nyms, for 'to Dance'," American Oriental Society
Journal, 36 (1916), p. 330ff

Although we will explore some evidence that this
sort of mourning dance played a role in early
Israelite ritual, the Israelite's eventually
rejected the mournful dance and its assumptions
and moved to a rejoiceful dance and a belief
that the world's problems were traceable to
people being dead to God and that the future of
the world thus depended on people's action of
reopening to God. The rejoiceful dance was a
way for people to open to God as indicated in
our earlier discussion of the prophets' use of
dance and the church's use of dance in repentance.
Thus, Israelite rejection of the mournful dance
and acceptance of the rejoiceful dance reflects
and effects a taking of responsibility for the
world. While other cultures contemporary to the
Israelite one recognized a joyful use of dance,[105]
Israel's exclusive association of dancing with
rejoicing is distinctive, expecially when seen
within the context of Canaanite practice outlined
in connection with Baal worship.

Traces of an early Israelite use of mournful
dance are evident in the Old Testament. The
pass-over is _pesach_ which we assume is derived

---

105. Haldar, _op. cit._, p. 60 notes that "the
Sumerian word for 'to dance' gu ud is the exact
equivalent of the Accadian rakadu, which also
means 'to rejoice.'"

from the leaping of the Lord at the initiation
of the Exodus (Exodus 12.11ff). Dr. C. H. Toy
argues that the name of this particular event
was derived from the sort of dance practiced in
the early celebration of the festival. Toy's
argument is bolstered by the derivation of the
general word for festival (chagag) from dance
(chagag). [106] Although Toy's derivation for
pesach is possible, no other instance of Israelite dance among dozens related in the Old
Testament is called pesach. [107] Even the dance
celebration led by Miriam at the Exodus (which
according to Toy's argument would be called
pesach if any dance would) is not pesach but the
mecholah (Exodus 15.20). Thus, either Dr. Toy's
argument is incorrect or evidence of the early
pesach type dancing has been eliminated as a
part of the general elimination of mourning
dance by those who were involved in the formalizing of the Old Testament Tradition. As the

---

106. C.H.Toy, "The Meaning of Pesach," Journal
of Biblical Literature, XVI, (1897), pp. 178-179.

107. There is a tradition of dance called "Biblical Pesach," but it's origin is uncertain and
unlikely to date back to antiquity. For this
dance, see Florence Freehof, Jews Are A Dancing
People, (San Francisco, 1954), p. 56.

Old Testament now stands, pesach is an instance
of God dancing mournfully at one time, not man
dancing mournfully again and again. The description of God's dance as a mournful one could be
in line with the explanations for the somewhat
subdued tone in which Jews are to celebrate
passover: one's happiness at freedom must be
conditioned by sadness for the killing of men --
even one's enemies. But that this attitude
prevailed at the time of the formation of the Old
Testament tradition could certainly be disputed
by instances of joyous dance that greeted Saul's
slaughter of thousands and David's slaughter of
ten thousands (I Samuel 29.5) and other such
victories.

The Hebrew name of Elisha's birth place is
another evidence of a mournful dance in Israel's
past: Abel-meholah (mourning dance). Jewish
commentators admit that this name derives from
the use of dance in mourning for the dead. But
these commentators assert that the dance itself
was not of a mournful type; they assert that
dance at a funeral signified a rejoicing and
hence a belief in a future life. [108] But this

---

108. Louis Ginzberg, The Legends of the Jews,
Philadelphia, 1938), VI, p. 343. The commentary
Ginzberg draws upon appears to be quite late--
after the Talmudic and Midrashic material--but
could stem from an earlier oral tradition.

argument rests of course on the fact that rejoicing and dancing were synonymous and excluded
mourning. Such an exclusive association of rejoicing and dancing was not necessarily established at the time of naming Abelmeholah.

There are other linguistic traces for a mournful
dance in Israel's past. In his etymological
study of terms for dance in the Old Testament,
Julian Morgenstern points out that hillu (sorrow)
and elehu (lamentation) could stem from the
principal term for dance (chul) which we have
noted is the infinitive of such nouns as machol
and mecholah: the terms generally used for dance
in the Old Testament. [109] But these and other
uses of chul for "sorrow" and "lamentation" are
nowhere explicitly or implicitly intertwined
with uses of chul for "dance". Another term
suggesting a connection between dancing and
mourning is nud which may mean skipping or mourning. But this term is not common in the Old
Testament; and in the one instance where nud is
used for dance, it results in joy (Jeremiah 48.27).

Examples of explicit rejection of any connection
between dancing and mourning and explicit affirmation of the connection of dancing with rejoicing

109. Morgenstern, op. cit., p. 332.

abound in the Old Testament. As early as the
tradition about Miriam's dance at the Exodus,
joy and dance come together. In the greeting of
Saul after David's victories over the Philistines,
joy (simchah) is associated with dancing
(mecholah) (I Samuel 18.6). Simchah is again
associated with machol in Psalm 30.11; and
mourning is explicitly contrasted to dancing:
"Thou hast turned for me my mourning into dancing:
thou hast put off my sackcloth, and girded me
with gladness." This same rejection of any
positive correlation between dancing and mourning
is evident in Jeremiah 31.13 where the dance
(machol) aids one to rejoice from sorrow.
Lamentation 5.15 reflects this same approach to
rejoicing: "The joy of our heart is ceased;
our dance (machol) is turned into mourning."
The contrasts of Ecclesiastes 3.4 reinforce the
foregoing distinctions: "A time to weep and a
time to laugh: a time to mourn, and a time to
dance" (raqad).

At the time of Jesus, dancing was still a literal
part of rejoicing and feasting as indicated by
his parable of the return of the son to the
father where the great joy and feasting included
dance (Luke 15.25). The continued contrasting
of dancing and mourning is evident in Jesus'
saying in Matthew 11.17 about the people's

90

different expectations of John the Baptist and
Jesus: "We piped to you and you did not dance;
we wailed, and you did not mourn." That dance
was understood by Jews as being the means to rejoice at the time of Jesus is suggested by our
comparison of Matthew 5.12 and Luke 6.23 in
chapter one. We have noted that the Jew would
know that "rejoice" meant "dance" as Matthew
Black pointed out: the word for rejoice in
Aramaic (which Jesus is assumed to have originally spoken) meant dance. [110]

Thus in accounts of Jesus rejoicing in the spirit
(Luke 10.21, etc.), we probably have pictures of
Jesus himself dancing. The connection of dancing
and rejoicing in Jewish practice around the time
of Jesus is indicated also by descriptions of
the celebration of the festival of booths at

---

110. Black, op. cit., p. 158. Although there is
no such linguistic connection between "dance"and
"joy" in Greek, the dynamics are universal
enough that Plato "proposes this impossible
etymology, striving to connect the Greek words
chara, 'joy' and choros, 'choral dance." Lillian
B. Lawler, The Dance in Ancient Greece, (Middle-
town, Connecticut, 1964), p. 14. The understanding of the connection of dance and joy is
also evident at the time of the translation in
the Septuagint (third and second centuries,B.C.)
when translating machol by in gaudium.

the Temple:

> He who has not seen the rejoicing at the
> place of the water-drawing has never seen
> rejoicing in his life. At the conclusion
> of the first day of the tabernacles they
> descended to the court of the women where
> they made a great enactment. ...Men of
> piety and good deeds used to dance before
> them with lighted torches in their hands
> and sing songs and praises. 111

Included as dancers in this tradition were the
most illustrious Jews of the time: Hillel the

---

111. Mishnah Sukkah 51a-b, The Talmud, op. cit.,
Mo'ed VI, p. 242. We would like to have many
more such explicit references to dancing in
Israelite and Christian worship; but as G. Henton
Davies has pointed out, dancing "was an activity
so common as not to require special mention."
"Dancing," The Interpreter's Dictionary of the
Bible, (Nashville, 1956), I, p. 760. The importance of our word study is that several words
suggested the presence of dance, such as "rejoice"
or the very word for "festival": "that the
religious dance constituted the principal
feature of every festival is shown by the history
of the word חגג ." Emil G. Hirsch, "Dance:
The Biblical Data," The Jewish Encyclopedia,
Isadore Singer, ed.,(New York, 1903). חג   or
חגג (hag or chagag) is rendered "dance
explicitly in I Samuel 30.16; elsewhere in the
Old Testament we may infer "dance" from
"festival" with some certainty.

Elder [112] and Simeon ben Gamaliel I. [113]
(Simeon was the grandson of Hillel, was the son
of the Gamaliel who taught Paul, was the father
of Gamaliel II who was the most prominent rabbi
at the close of the first century, and was the
great grandfather of R. Judah Hanasi "the Prince,"
who is credited with formalizing the Talmud.)

The use of dance as a religious practice declined
at the end of Sanhedrin and Temple authority for
several reasons -- most prominent of which was
the Jewish trauma at being powerless and finally
exiled. This sort of trauma seems also to have
appeared in the earlier exile as described in
Psalm 137.4: "How shall we sing the Lord's
song in a foreign land?" The loss of the sense
that people could do anything about their
condition led to the decline of singing and
dancing. (Gen Gabinius is credited with ending
the authority of the Sanhedrin in the middle of
the first century; and "when the Sanhedrin
ceased to function, song ceased from the places

---

112. Gemara Sukkah, The Talmud, op. cit., Mo'ed
VI, p. 253.
113. Ibid.

of feasting.") [114]

The exception to this general pattern of mourning at powerlessness and exile was at weddings where mourning gave way to rejoicing and dancing. [115] (A wedding with the promise of children was a time to celebrate the hope for the rebirth of

---

114. A. Cohen, trans., Mishnah Sotah 48a, The Talmud, op. cit., Nashim, p. 256. By the time of Raba B. Hanin (c. A.D. 350), the elimination of dancing from sabbath and festivals was explained by arguing that dancing might lead to the repairing of instruments which was forbidden on such occasions as labor: Mishnah Bezah 36b and 30a, The Talmud, op. cit., Mo'ed VI, p. 154. Another explanation for the decline of dance is traced to the decline of all public forms of Jewish life resulting from a desire not to be conspicuous in the lands of exile: B. Zemach, "The Beginning of Jewish Dance," The Jewish Dance, Fred Berk, ed., (New York, 1960), p.16.

115. Rabbis are reported to have even led dancing with the brides after the fall of the Sanhedrin in the following records: T. Tarphon, (c. A.D. 115), Aboth de Rabbi Nathan, ed., S. Schechter, (London, 1887), vers. I, XLI, 67a; R. Judah ben El'ai, (c. A.D. 145), Gemara Kethuboth 17a, The Talmud, op. cit., Nashim III p. 93; Samuel bar Issac, (c. A.D. 280), Peah 15d, Manual of the Aramaic Language of the Palestinian Talmud, J. T. Marshall, ed., (Leyden, 1929), p. 133.

the Jewish State. We will explore the connection
of dancing with this hope later in this chapter.)
Weddings continued to be the occasions for Jewish
dancing through the middle ages so that the
halls in which the week-long wedding celebrations
were held became known as dance halls. [116] In
line with the assertions in this paper about the
connection of a people's sense of possibility
and responsibility and their use of a rejoiceful
dance, it is interesting to note that for the
Hassidim (who revived dance as a regular religious
practice for their movement which spread through
Eastern Europe in the eighteenth century) the
dance was "a conscious attempt to create human
joyousness out of misery." [117] Similarly the
rise of dance in modern Israel and Zionist
movements around the world coincided with this
same reemergence of a people's recognition of
their possibility to change the world. [118] Hava
Nagila, the folk tune and folk dance which expresses this modern Jewish spirit means "Come,
let us rejoice!".

---

116. Israel Abrahams, Jewish Life in the Middle
Ages, (New York, 1896), pp. 196, 380-381.

117. Dvora Lapson, "The Chassidic Dance," Berk,
op. cit., p. 21.

118. David Macarov, Youth and Chalutziut Dept.,
Jewish Agency, Jerusalem, "Introduction,"
Jewish Dance, Berk, op. cit.

CHRISTIAN REJOICEFUL DANCE
AND RECOGNITION OF PROGRESS

Jesus appears to be fully in line with this
Jewish understanding of dancing when he says in
the passage we have already examined: "Leap for
Joy." The Christian church continued to use
dance to create greater joy in worship. In a
work credited to Justin Martyr (A.D. 100-165),
we see the following scene of the use of dance
in Christian worship:

> It is not for the little ones to sing
> alone, but rather together with musical
> instruments and dancing and rattles, just
> in the same way as one enjoys songs and
> similar music in church. 119

To enjoy the songs and music in church, one
danced. (Of course dancing continued to be an
expression of joy in worship as Eusebius
attests; [120] but in this chapter we are more

---

119. "Questions and Responses to the Orthodox,"
(In Latin and Greek by Otto, ed., Saint Justin
Philosopher and Martyr, Works, III, pt.2), Eng.
trans., Taylor, A Time To Dance, op. cit., pp.
72-73. This work may be the product of a late
4th century writer, possibly Diodorus, bishop of
Tarsus (ca.391), and teacher of John Chrysostom.

120. Eusebius, op. cit., pp. 51, 325. In an expression of joyous thanks, Christians engaged in
dancing and hymn singing to God when Constantine
was victorious over Licinius.

concerned with a people's use of dance in connection with their ability to create and affect
their condition.)

Tripudium, the most common dance step used in
Christian processions symbolized the thesis of
this chapter: there is a strong positive
correlation between the use of dance in worship
and a people's consciousness of their ability
to change and affect their condition in spite
of apparent setbacks.   In Latin "tripudium"
means three step and came to mean jubilation
paralleling the similar development which we
noted of the word "joy" from "dance" in the
Aramaic.   (In the late middle ages tripudium's
literal meaning and practice as dance was suppressed in the general suppression of dance
already detailed; and tripudium came to mean
just jubilation.   But in the few places where
dance processions survived in Christian worship
into this century (as in Echternach, Luxembourg)
tripudium remained the style of processing.   In
this dance step, one takes three steps forward
and then one step back, three steps forward and
then one step back .... The significance of this
movement was to symbolize the progress in health
and welfare not only of the individual but also
of the whole church and community.   (Setbacks
were thus to be seen within the context of

continued forward progress.) [121] On the current
scene of Christian social movements, marches
for civil rights and peace are persistent signs
of a people's faith and hope that they can
change the conditions of the world even in face
of setbacks and overwhelming odds against them.

A people's belief that they can shape the material world into a better place is based in turn
on their belief that the material world is not
inherently evil but rather is potentially good
as God's creation. First let us see how dancing
in Jewish and Christian practice has been based
on a world view (and has helped bring others to
a world view) that the material world is potentially good and within a people's possibility
and responsibility to uplift. Then let us turn
to movements for modern church worship to develop
this worldview in our congregations.

JEWISH DANCE AND RECOGNITION OF RESPONSIBILITY

If one follows Julian Morgenstern's argument for
the etymology of three Hebrew terms for dance,
one realizes the role of dance in the process
by which a people came to see the physical world

---

121. Backman, op. cit., passim.

(harvest, land, etc.) as appropriated from God for human use and development. This process was based on "dance" and rendered the objects "profane." By "profane" no negative moral judgment is implied. "Profane" simply meant that the objects were usable by people rather than being the exclusive province of God. Morgenstern asserts that etymologically "profane" (<u>chalal</u>) as well as a host of related terms are derived from dance (<u>chil</u>). Morgenstern notes that most lexicographers have taken pains to distinguish these two terms and their derivatives; and Morgenstern admits that the similarities of these terms and their derivatives could be coincidence if this were the only case of similarity between terms for dance and profane. But Morgenstern shows a connection between another Hebrew term for dance (<u>chagag</u>) and words for parts of the vineyard associated with the profaning as well as a connection for terms for dance and profane in Arabic. From the following sort of reasoning, Morgenstern carries the reader along to the conclusions just outlined above:

> the word חִלּוּלָא , 'a dancing-place in the vineyard', could never have developed from חִל(החול), 'to dance,' paralleling precisely the development of נָחֹל , from חֹל , had not some deep meaning and purpose attached to the general rite of

dancing, and particularly of dancing in
the vineyards. 122

Morgenstern's argument is convincing enough to
this writer; so, we conclude that dance is
intimately connected to the Israelite's real
use of the world:

> Possibly because the offering of the
> taboo-sacrifice marked the beginning of
> the profane, and therefore real use of the
> tabooed object, חלל came to mean in the
> Hiphil, 'to begin.' 123

Dancing by women in the vineyards as an exciting
part of their initiation from virginity into
matrimony (through the profaning process into
real use) is described by R. Simeon ben Gamaliel
I as the great days of joy each year at the
fifteenth of Ab and the day of atonement when
the daughters of Jerusalem went out into the
vineyards with dancing and went through this
process which led to marriage. 124 An exploration of examples of dancing with the bride
reveals the deeper dynamic of dance to celebrate
a commitment to the world and to uplift the

---

122. Morgenstern, op. cit., p. 324.

123. Morgenstern, op. cit., p. 328.

124. R. Simeon ben Gamaliel I, Mishnah Ta'anith
26b, The Talmud, op. cit., Mo'ed VII, p. 139.

person. R. Judah ben Zabina (c. A.D. 345) is
associated with the following story which
illustrates the dance in connection with this
commitment. Pharaoh had decreed the death of
all male Hebrew children; and Amram had responded
by separating from his wife so no children would
be born and then killed. Miriam criticized him
saying:

> Father, thy decree is worse than Pharaoh's
> decree. The Egyptians aim to destroy only
> the male children, but thou includest the
> girls as well. Pharaoh deprives his
> victims of life in this world, but thou
> preventest children from being born, and
> this deprivest them of future life, too.
> Accordingly, Amram stood publicly under
> the wedding canopy with his divorced wife
> Jochebed while Aaron and Miriam danced
> about it, and the angels proclaimed, "Let
> the mother of children be joyful!" 125

Aaron and Miriam danced with joy for the renewed
commitment. The association of dance with fer-
tility and children implies a commitment to the
world and future hope; for in having children
one assumes a responsibility and commitment to
the world with all it's risks. The first
commandment to people from God is to be fruitful

---

125. R. Judah ben Zebina, Sotah 12a, The Talmud,
op. cit., Nashim VI, p. 60. We have done such a
ring dance around couples in weddings; and we
have danced "Mayim, Mayim" around the family
and child at Baptisms.

and multiply in the world for which the people
are committed to care. (Genesis 1.28).

The use of dance to point out and uplift the
best in a person is suggested in the following
story of an encounter between the schools of
Shammai and Hillel:

> Our rabbis taught: How does one dance
> before the bride? Beth Shammai says: "the
> bride as she is." And Beth Hillel says
> "Beautiful and gracious bride!" Beth
> Shammai said to Beth Hillel: "If she is
> lame and blind, does one say of her,
> 'beautiful and gracious bride'? Whereas
> the Torah said: 'Keep thee far from a
> false matter.'" Said Beth Hillel to Beth
> Shammai, "According to your words, if one
> made a bad purchase in the market should
> one praise it in his eyes or depreciate
> it? Surely one should praise it in his
> eyes. Therefore the Sages say, 'Always,
> should the disposition of man be pleasant
> with people.'" 126

CHRISTIAN DANCE AND RECOMMITMENT TO THE WORLD

It is revealing that many of those who have difficulty accepting dance in Christian worship also
have difficulty with communion and the other

---

126. Gemara Kethuboth I, 17a, The Talmud,
op. cit., Nashim III, pp. 92-93.
127. C.F. Footnote 115.

sacraments in worship. Stewart Headlam noted
this same phenomenon in the late nineteenth
century in England:

> The art of dancing, ...perhaps more than
> all other arts, is an outward and visible
> sign of an inward and spiritual grace,
> ordained by the Word of God himself, as a
> means whereby we receive the same and a
> pledge to assure us thereof; and it has
> suffered even more than the other arts
> from the utter anti-sacramentalism of the
> British philistia. Your Manichean Protest-
> ant, and your superfine rationalist, reject
> the dance as worldly, frivolous, sensual
> and so forth; and your dull, stupid sen-
> sualist sees legs, and grunts with some
> satisfaction; but your sacramentalist
> knows something worth more than both of
> these. He knows what perhaps the dancer
> herself may be partially unconscious of,
> that we live now by faith and not by sight,
> and that the poetry of dance is the ex-
> pression of unseen spiritual grace. 128

Dancing and the sacraments lead to the same
realization: concern for the material world
(on which we are dependent) and for its increased
intention toward higher forms of activity,
complexity, and community. The theologians of
the Orthodox Church have most fully developed
the implications of the incarnation and our

---

128. Stewart Headlam, an article in The Church
Reformer, 1884, reprinted in Margaret Taylor's
A Time To Dance, (Boston, 1967), p. 108.

resulting sacramental religion. As Nicholas
Zernov concludes, "The whole growth of modern
civilization is rooted in Eucharistic worship."[129]
It is not the purpose of this paper to duplicate
the orthodox work which is increasingly available
in the West and which has its counterparts in
current Western thinking. [130]

But it is crucial for the continued growth of
civilization that western people (who are now
tempted to resolve their tensions by escape from
the world through use of drugs) take the incarnation as their model and become recommitted to
the material dimension of the world.

One way for this recommitment to take place is
through dance. A leading Orthodox spokesman has
called for dance in Christian worship to achieve
just such a recommitment in the western world.
A. M. Allchin, secretary of the Society of St.
Albans and St. Sergius (the ecumenical movement
of Anglican and Orthodox), has written that the
Shaker worship (largely dance) was the most
orthodox worship in the West; [131] for such
worship recognized "that God is made known to

129. Nicholas Zernov, Orthodox Encounter, op. cit.
p. 75.
130. Cf. Conrad Bonifazi, A Theology of Things,
(Philadelphia, 1967).
131. A. M. Allchin, "Introduction," Sacrament and
Image, (London, 1967), pp. 10-11.

man, as he is, a body-soul unity, and not to his
mind or spirit alone." [132] With this realization of themselves as a body-soul unity,
people should seek the solution to their problems
in the way outlined in chapter three, not through
escape from the world but rather through work
in the World.

In defining sacrament, William Temple writes, "it
is a spritual utilization of a material object
whereby a spiritual result is effected." [133]
The effects of dancing recounted in these chapters
include the growth of solidarity and commitment
to all in the world and the movement toward
greater activity, and complexity, and community.
The foregoing are spiritual results when one
properly understands the usage of "spirit" as
outlined in chapter three. The dance brings
movement and direction to the body and so
transforms it. Dance is not separate from the
body but is more than just body (not materially
but intentionally). Thus, dance is to body
as spirit is to body: one and inseparable but
more.

---

132. Ibid., p. 8. But the shaker dance and theology is actually anti-incarnational (C.F. The
entry on Edward Deming Andrews in the select
annotated bibliography.)
133. William Temple, "The Sacramental Universe,"
Nature, Man and God, (London, 1935), p. 491.

As we come to understand Christ's action of
incarnation and communion as a force toward
growth of activity, complexity, and community,
we come to recognize not only a dimension of the
Word but also an implication for the direction
of our words and movements in worship services.
Elizabeth Sewell has pointed out the function
of language most revealing in calling Christ
"the Word":

> We are curiously inclined to think and
> speak as if the mind thought somewhere away
> from itself, and the body inside and through
> which it is doing its thinking could be
> ignored. Grammar does not treat language
> processes in this way. It treats them as
> bodily, and as sexual. There are general
> references to bodily life, such as the fact
> that verbs have "moods" and "voices", but
> the majority of references of this sort
> are to bodily fertility, as if it were the
> chief contribution of the body to language
> activity and of thought; in "copula" and
> "conjugation" in grammatical terminology,
> and most of all in the phenomenon of gender
> in nouns, where not necessarily just the
> object referred to but the noun itself will
> have a gender. 134

One effect of sacraments and dance in worship
services is to remind us of the bodily base of

---

134. Elizabeth Sewell, The Orphic Voice: Poetry
and Natural History, (London, 1961), p. 35.

all life. The dancing and the eating in worship
make us aware of our material nature and hence
our solidarity with and commitment to the world
(common matter including people).   By recognizing our dependence on matter, we realize our
solidarity with its fate and our commitment to
its preservation. By recognizing our own dependence, we should recognize the similar
dependence of others and our common cause with
them. Also from the foregoing, we should
recognize the Word as a unifying agent and role
of words for the same quasi sexual purpose.
Thus is set the standard by which preaching,
dancing and any other activity in worship should
be judged: they are acceptable if they have the
effect of leading to greater community and
commitment to the world in its growth.

Toward this recommitment, A. M. Allchin notes
that the Western attraction to African music and
dance is a sign of hope; "for Africans do not
seem to have lost that easiness, that at-homeness
is their bodies which we know we lack." [135] The
use of the body and dance are normative in black
worship. Whites interested in black and white
together today or someday should begin preparing
white congregations to move; so that in integration

---

135. Allchin, op. cit., p. 10.

blacks will not have to leave their bodies behind
as they have had to do in the past whenever
entering white worship services. Blacks are in
a position to give the great gift of renewal of
the body and worship to whites. In one of the
most hopeful passages in modern literature,
Eldridge Cleaver first identifies a key problem
for twentieth century people and then notes
the role of dance in the process of "Convalescence"
from Soul On Ice:

> Song and dance are, perhaps, only a little
> less old than man himself. It is with his
> music and dance, the recreation through
> art of the rhythms suggested by and implicit
> in the tempo of his life and cultural
> environment, that man purges his soul of
> the tensions of daily strife and maintains
> his harmony in the universe. In the
> increasingly mechanized, automated, cyber-
> nated environment of the modern world --
> a cold, bodiless world of wheels, smooth
> plastic surfaces, tubes, pushbuttons,
> transistors, computers, jet propulsion,
> rockets to the moon, atomic energy -- man's
> need for affirmation of his biology has
> become that much more intense. He feels
> need for a clear definition of where his
> body ends and the machine begins, where
> man ends and the extensions of man begin.
> This great mass hunger, which transcends
> national or racial boundaries, recoils from
> the subtle subversions of the mechanical
> environment which modern technology is
> creating faster than man, with his present
> savage relationship to his fellow men, is
> able to receive and assimilate. This is
> the central contradiction of the twentieth

century; and it is against this backdrop
that America's attempt to unite its Mind
with its Body, to save its soul, is taking
place. 136

The history of America in the years following the pivotal Supreme Court edict should
be a record of the convalescence of the
nation. And upon investigation we should
be able to see the whites grappling with
their unfamiliar and alienated Bodies, and
the blacks attempting to acquire and assert
a mind of their own. The record, I think,
is clear and unequivocal. The bargain
which seems to have been struck is that the
whites have had to turn to the blacks for
a clue on how to swing with the Body,
while the blacks have had to turn to the
whites for the secret of the Mind. It was
Chubby Checker's mission, bearing the Twist
as good news, to teach the whites, whom
history had taught to forget, how to shake
their asses again. 137

Let us turn to ways to spread this good news to
those in our congregation.

JOYFUL DANCE FOR RESPONSIBLE
CHRISTIAN WORSHIP TODAY

Let us explore several simple dance practices to

---

136. Eldridge Cleaver, Soul On Ice, (New York,
1968), pp. 202-203.
137. Ibid., pp. 192-193.

help people realize that Christian worship is
for the purpose of uplifting the material world.
Then let us explore ways to encourage people in
their faith that this uplifting is possible even
when there are setbacks or seemingly overwhelming
odds against this work.

From the time they take communion to the recession, the Orthodox stand to symbolize the
stregthening effects of communion. That communion
is directed toward the physical regeneration of
ourselves and the material world could be easily
emphasized by this practice of standing. In
Catholic services whenever "The Lord be with
you" is said, the people stand in realization
of the strengthening effect of God operating in
and through them. To further develop this
understanding during the praying of the Lord's
Prayer, the people could be led to raise their
own arms and hands on "Thy Kingdom Come, Thy
Will Be Done, On Earth as it is in Heaven."
By raising and looking at their own hands during
this prayer, the people may come to see their
hands as God's hands and the media for the
mission of uplifting the world. By holding the
hands of others during this movement, the people
realize also that theirs are not the only hands
struggling to bring God's Kingdom. As a prayer
at meals or as a response during the reading of

110

psalms in worship, the following pattern may be
employed: after each line or phrase of the
psalm is read by a leader, the people could
raise their arms while saying or singing "Praise
the Lord." (The people could lower their arms
as the leader reads the next line and then raise
their arms again during the next "Praise the
Lord." Holding hands throughout the whole
process of raising and lowering and raising
again adds the sense of dedication to uplift each
other and the material world as our proper
response to and praise of God.) Psalm 147 is
particularly appropriate for this practice of
prayer at meals or on preparation for communion. [138] A carrying of the Bible into the
world at the head of the recession of Minister,
choir, and people is especially effective to
remind all that what we do in worship has to do
with uplifting the world.

To help people see the possibilities, even when
the setbacks are most obvious, one may lead all
in moving to the tripudium step described earlier
in this chapter. As suggested in chapter one,
singing "Amen" or "ain't Gonna Let Nobody Turn

138. Conducted by this author and John Burke,
minister of music for 1st Congregational Church,
Berkeley, California.

Round" while moving to this step heightens the
meaning of perseverance and hope. (People may
call out the sign of hope and the setbacks as
they take the steps; for example, in one liberal
church in California when we did this step,
the people chanted "Cranston, Tunney, Riles,"
on the three forward steps, and "Reagan" on the
backstep.) A step similar in dynamics to the
tripudium is one used in many black churches.
This step is a modification of the African
high-life. In the African high-life one moves
forward on the right foot, draws the left foot
toward the right heel, then steps forward with
the left foot and draws the right foot to the
left heel. In the black church use of the high-
life, one steps forward on the right foot,
draws the left foot up to the right heel, returns
the left foot to its initial position, and then
draws the left foot forward again to a position
by the right heel; then one steps forward on the
left foot and moves the right foot in the
forward-backward-forward pattern just performed
by the left foot. Many blacks use this sequence
of steps in processing into the nave. As with
the tripudium step, this modified high-life
step leads one to see the marking of time in the
larger context of forward progress. And the
step is sometimes done with a stomping of the
feet that is quite liberating.

During the Good Friday-Easter period, this dynamic of dance is most appropriate. To help
people see the crucifixion in the context of
the resurrection, we devised the following
pageant with use of dance and other media.
Four weeks in advance of the Good Friday services
in which four churches participated, we began
circulating among the churches a life-sized
wooden cross. The cross became a part of the
worship in each church for a week's period of
time. People were told that the cross would
be used in the Good Friday worship and were
encouraged to write of their hopes in prayers
which were then taped to the cross. By Good
Friday the cross was covered with many prayers
not only from members of the four congregations
at home and abroad, but also from people in the
community at large who had sent prayers through
the mail. 139

After a standard Good Friday worship service,
we moved into a more moving worship in which the
people in the congregation became the crowd at
the crucifixion. The people were instructed to

---

139. The four participating churches were
Arlington Community Church, El Cerrito Methodist
Church, Mira Vista United Church of Christ, and
Northminster Presbyterian Church where the
worship service was held.

respond to the figure of Christ carrying the cross in whatever way they felt appropriate. We began the drama by having the minister take the role of Pontius Pilate in asking the crowd, "Whom would you have me free, Barabbas or Jesus?" Many in the crowd were silent, but a few cried out "Give us Barabbas!" Then to Pilate's question, "Then what would you have me do with this man Jesus?", several cried out "Crucify him!" while many remained silent. At that moment we turned out the lights, turned on the electronic music (Lewin-Richter Study No. 1) which established the mood for Good Friday, and began showing a film strip of Barnett Newman's Fourteen Stations of the Cross on a screen at the back of the nave. [140] From the back of the nave, one person whom I had trained in advance, began

140. Lewin-Richter "Study No. 1" is available on "Electronic Music" Vox Productions, TV 3400S. The Barnett Newman "Stations of the Cross" are available in a multi-media kit "Creative Arts in Reconciliation", (Friendship Press, New York, 1969). Those who spontaneously join in carrying the cross could come forward with it and then be motioned to kneel or settle down at the base of the cross for the crucifixion. Mrs. Thom Jones suggests the importance of allowing the people who respond to follow the cross all the way forward for meaningful participation.

struggling to carry the huge cross down the
center aisle of the nave as all joined in enacting
the fourteen stations ("The First Fall," "Christ
Meets Mary," "Simon Helps Carry The Cross," etc.)
while I moved as a director among the people:
at one point I encouraged several women to be
Mary and go to Jesus; at another point, I encouraged several men to act as Simeon and go to
help carry the cross. In advance we had picked
several people to be ready to hold Jesus to the
cross and pantomime the driving in of nails
while pounding on the floor to make the crucifixion more realistic. Many helped carry the
body from the cross to entombment at the base
of the altar.

In the introduction to this dramatization, the
only instruction we had given for everyone to
follow was that at the time of the entombment
all were to die symbolically with Christ by
closing their eyes and bowing their heads (if
they were still in the pews) or by closing their
eyes and prostrating themselves on the floor
(if they were in the aisles or chancel area).
The people were instructed to remain in these
positions until the risen Christ came to them,
opened their eyes, and raised them. At the
moment of their resurrection, they were to join
Christ in singing the Stanza of "Christ the Lord

Is Risen Today" which reads:

> Soar we now where Christ has led, Alleluia!
> Following our exalted Head, Alleluia!
> Made like Him like Him we rise, Alleluia!
> Ours the cross, the grave, the skies,
>   Alleluia!

After the entombment, the tape recording of
electronic music and the remaining lights were
turned off. The person taking the role of Christ
remained silent for a few minutes which seemed
to be hours. Then Christ rose and began softly
humming the foregoing song and raising others.
They in turn raised others as the singing swelled
to a triumphant chorus. The figure of Christ
ended the service by leading all in a joyful
quick-paced procession around the church and
finally outside into the sunshine. Once during
the foregoing dance sequence in worship, a woman
burst into tears when there was the sound of
pounding the nails at the cross. In the personal
counselling that followed immediately, she
shared the fact that her father's funeral had
been held ten years earlier, but she had not
been able to attend. She had never done her
grief work; and only then because of the dance
was the emotion evoked. Dance helps in this way.
But the incident suggests the wisdom of having
someone available to do counseling during and
after worship services that include powerful

116

dance sequences.

Joyous dancing should be employed at Christian
funerals to testify to the faith that death is
not the end, but rather resurrection follows.
Few Christian funerals testify to such faith
today; but joyous dancing was characteristic of
early Christian funerals which celebrated the
true birthday not death of a person. To help
children and others express this faith, the
minister might lead the children in playing "Ring
around the Rosie" at a funeral. Children will
enter into this game with the joy intended.
Then the minister could explain that this dance
game originated in early English Christian
funeral services. "Rosie" signified the plague
itself: the rose color left on the cheeks of
the victim. There were flowers and ashes typical
of the funeral (but the English say "ahchew,
ahchew" - the first sign of being taken with the
plague); and all fell down to symbolize the fact
that all will die. All are going to die; but
this is not the end. Thus, let us dance the
song with joy at a funeral.

To allow joy to take hold in worship, we need
to allow very rapid movement as well as slow
steps. Having several concentric circles during
the singing of carols and other hymns aids this

movement; for children and others wishing to
move quickly can form the inner circle while
those wishing to walk or stand may form the
outer circle. An especially effective way of
dancing to "Shalom," at the end of the worship
or before communion as the peace, is to have
those in the outer circle face inward and those
in the inner circle face outward -- all facing
and passing those in the outer circle while
singing "Shalom". (This was designed by Margaret
Chaney).

Having the minister or members of the choir or
whoever wishes sing the lyrics of many hymns to
one or two individuals will increase the intensity of the lyrics and bring them to life. The
choir of Skyline United Church, Oakland, California, sings the benediction or the last hymn
of dismissal after positioning one of the choir
members at the end of each pew. From this
position, the choir member looks into the eyes
of each person in that pew as all choir members
sing the hymn.

Let us conclude this section with the advice and
hope given us by Hasidic Rabbi Zalman Schachter.
After leading us in dance at Pacific School of
Religion, Zalman concluded, "Now you will be
going back to your churches and temples where

you will often find yourselves trappped in pews
or for psychological reasons unable to dance
joyfully down the aisles during the hymns or
sermons; but one thing you can do, even sitting
in the pews, is ... wiggle your toes. Go ahead;
do it. Wiggling your toes, you begin smiling;
and that is what will happen. You will be
sitting in your pew smiling throughout the hymn
and sermon. Then the person sitting next to
you will ask, "Why are you smiling?" And you
will whisper to him, "I'm wiggling my toes."
And soon he will begin wiggling his toes; and
soon everyone will be wiggling their toes. And
they will throw the pews out; and all will dance
together! That day will be the second coming
for you; the first for us!"

CHAPTER V

DANCING AND REDEDICATION

Dancing has been used in Christian worship to
reveal God and those close to God as active as
well as to help people identify themselves with
this active moving God through their own movement. This identification through movement was
used to increase the people's Christian intentions and transform these intentions into actions.
We will study first the motif of God and God's
followers as dancing, then the role of dancing
in increasing Christian intentions and transforming them into actions, and finally the ways
to use dance for these purposes in worship
today.

THE IMPLICATIONS OF A MOVING
GOD FOR MOVING PEOPLE

The behavior a people ascribe to their God guides
their own behavior. In light of this dynamic,
Samuel Jackson notes a transformation that
occurred in the Israelite's behavior:

> sacred processions fell into disuse in
> worship of Yahweh after the ark was

transferred to Solomon's Temple. [141]

When the people ceased to view God as moving,
the motivation for their own movement ceased.
Of course some dancing persisted in Jewish
worship as we have seen; but the concept of God
at rest in the Temple provided little motivation
for people's activity in worship or in the rest
of life. Recognizing the importance of creating
an active image of God for the fostering of an
activity among the people, let us explore
materials to help us see God and God's followers
as moving.

God is envisioned as moving and leading Israelite
movement throughout the Old Testament. He leaps
at the initiation of the exodus and leads the
people through the wilderness. God's ark moves
and leads the people into battle in the conquest
of the promised land. Later Jewish writers
characterized many of God's acts for Israel as
dance: the dance of the angels before Jacob
as he left Laban and faced danger, the dance
provided the ancestors at the opening of the Red
Sea, the dance provided for Elisha in the inci-
dents in II Kings VI, 15ff, and the dance to be

---

141. Samuel Jackson, "Dancing," The Schaff-
Herzog Encyclopedia of Religious Knowledge,
(New York, 1908).

provided by the Lord in the time to come. [142]
In chapter two we have already noted the numerous
passages in Talmud and Midrash where the future
is visualized with God leading the righteous in
dance. Similar scenes are envisaged in Christian literature: In describing the garden of
heaven for his small son, Luther saw "a beautiful
meadow, which was arranged for a dance." [143]

Jesus Christ is pictured as the leader of the
dance in the Acts of John. The long Hymn of
Jesus ritual in this gnostic text calls for the
people to respond by circling the dancing figure
of Christ. Jesus commands his followers,
"Answer to my dancing. See thyself in Me who
speak and dancing what I do ..." [144] In the
works of the fourteenth century, Wycliff pictures Christ as one who "led the dance of
love." [145] The hymns of the fifteenth century

142. Song of Songs VII, 1, 2, The Midrash,
op. cit., IX, pp. 275-277.

143. van der Leeuw, op. cit., p.

144. G. R. Mead, The Sacred Dance in Christendom,
"Quest Reprint Series," No. 2, (London, 1926),
pp. 66-67.

145. Thomas Arnold, ed., Selected Works,
(Oxford, 1869), II, p. 360.

Hildesheim mass contribute to this same dynamic
vision:

> Lord Jesus dances first of all.
> He leads the bride by the hand.
> He it is who jubilates.
> Jubilus is his name.
> Blessed he who jubilates.
> The soul grows warm in memory
> And filled with heavenly food.   146

Most recently, Sidney Carter has taken one of
the basic melodies used by the Shakers in their
dance worship and has changed the lyrics of the
chorus to identify Jesus Christ as "Lord of the
Dance:"

> Dance then wherever you may be;
> I am the Lord of the Dance, said he,
> And I'll lead you all wherever you may be.
> And I'll lead you all in the dance,
> said he.   147

The rest of Carter's lyrics describe the birth,
life, death and resurrection of Christ as dance.

The whole of creation has been envisioned as
dancing in response to God.   The first verse of

---

146. Backman, op. cit., p. 88.
147. Taylor, A Time To Dance, op. cit., p. 128.

Carter's reads, "I danced in the morning when
the world was begun; and I danced in the moon
and the stars and the sun ..." [148] Origen
(A.D. 185-254) described the stars and heavens
as dancing in response to God. [149] And the
dance of angels to evoke our imitation was
common in earlier church hymns and sermons. [150]

As we have already noted in chapter three, Dante
describes the angels and all who are close to
God as in constant motion.

As Christ and the heavens and angels move in
response to God's movement, so the church is to
respond by moving. We have already noted in
chapter two that the mass itself has been described as dance. Menestrier (a seventeenth
century French Jesuit), revealed a function and
meaning of praesul (bishop) and choir as seen

---

148. Ibid.

149. Origen,"De Principis" vii 5, Taylor, op. cit.
p. 74.

150. Cf. Clement of Alexandria, (A.D. 150-216),
"Exhortation to the Heathen," 12:119 (1-2), 120
(1), Migne, P. Gr., op. cit., 8, col. 239, Eng.
trans., Backman, op. cit., p. 19; Gregory (the
Wonder Worker), "Four Sermons," I. Migne, P.Gr.,
op. cit., 10, col. 1146, 1154, Eng. Trans.,
Backman, op. cit., p. 22; Basil, "Epistle" I:2,
Migne, P.Gr., op. cit., 32, col. 226, Eng.
trans., Backman, op. cit., p. 24.

through the original use of these terms in dance.
"Praesul" meant "dance leader" and "choir" meant
"dancing harmonious group." [151] Ted Shawn
records a similar though less certain origin
of prelate from premier danseur. [152] The
adoption of these terms for the leaders of the
mass reveals the purpose of the mass, bishop and
choir to move the people into action.

Dancing by the believer is symbolic of his active
response to God in life. [153] Through the
believer's response to God's activity, all of
the material world is activated toward God as
indicated in a hymn by Gregory the Wonder Worker
-- a hymn which pictures John the Baptist's
response to Christ:

> Dance with me, Jordan River, and leap with
> me, and set thy waves in rhythm,
> for thy maker has come to thee in body. 154

---

151. Fr. Menestrier, Des Ballets Anciens et
Modernes, (Paris, 1682).

152. Ted Shawn, "Religious Use of Dance,"
Religious Symbolism, Frederick Johnson, ed.,
(New York, 1955), p. 151.

153. Jacapone da Todi, a Franciscan monk of the
13th century, speaks of dance in this way:
Taylor, op. cit., p. 89.

154. Gregory Thaumaturgus, Hom.iv, (De Christi
Bapt.), Eng. trans., Taylor, op. cit., p. 74.

THE INCREASE OF INTENTIONS AND
TRANSFORMATION INTO ACTION

Dance has been used throughout Jewish history
to intensify the sense of community and to transform communal purpose into action. This dynamic
is obvious in the earliest period of communal
action under Joshua at Jericho, in the prophetic
use of dance, at the height of Israelite power
under David, and in the revival of Jewish community in the modern state of Israel. We will
explore the role of dance in each manifestation
of communal and military strength. This use of
dance in worldly activity could serve as a model
for strengthening modern political movements as
we take seriously the world and our task to
transform the world.

In Joshua 6 is pictured the military use of a
procession around and around Jericho. There may
be elements of consecration involved in this
circling as Oesterley suggests. [155] But this
writer assumes that the circling had the added
effect of increasing the Israelite community's
sense of intention and aiding the transformation
of that intention into action.

---

155. Oesterley, op. cit., p. 93.

The power of movement to lead individuals to
forget personal affairs and join communal activity has been noted already in the prophet's use
of dance and its effect upon Saul and his
messengers (I Samuel 19.18ff). The role of
dance in increasing intensity and transforming
intention into action may also be seen in the
earlier encounter of Saul with the prophetic
band. In the account in I Samuel 10, the following order of events is depicted. Samuel tells
Saul that when he (Saul) dances with the prophets,
he will be changed into another man (verse 6).
Before this transformation has taken place, Saul
leaves Samuel to go to the prophets; and at this
departing, God gives Saul another heart. In
Hebrew, "heart" often signifies a people's
intention; [156] so that in this passage Saul
felt a new intention. Yet, Hans Hertzberg has
noted that something remained which was later
fulfilled when Saul became "another man:" for
Hertzberg sees the change of heart as "readiness
not conversion." [157] The change of heart could

156. Aubrey Johnson, The Vitality of the Individual in the Thought of Ancient Israel, (Cardiff,
1949), p. 77ff.
157. Hans Hertzberg, I and II Samuel: A
Commentary, (Philadelphia, 1960), p. 86.

be a change on the rational level only (the heart
is the center of man's thinking in Israelite
understanding). Becoming "another man" could
indicate a greater dimension of emotional
involvement. We must be careful in making such
distinctions so as not to suggest any sort of
dualism in the person which would be totally
alien to the Israelite spirit. The change of
heart involved the whole person. The change into
another person probably involved a more all
embracing change. Dance had a function in
bringing about this greater transformation. One
can imagine the same function of dance in the
military use at Jericho.

The communal result of dance contributes to
greater power and activity as best illustrated
in David's use of dance for military purposes.
Cyrus Gordon suggested this Davidic use of dance
in drawing parallels between David and a compar-
able military genius and user of dance, Tyraeus
of Spartica (c. 650 B.C.). [158] Gordon points
out the similar Davidic use of song and poetry
for purposes of military instruction (cf. Psalm
60). That an army could gain a sense of comrad-
ship, coordination, and increased intensity of
purpose by dancing or marching is the experience

158. Cyrus Gordon, op. cit., pp. 46-49.

of anyone who has been in or close to a parade.

This same use of dance has served modern Israel
well in evoking a sense of community and drawing
together many Jews from many different lands
as we noted in chapter two. The reappearance
of dance and the revitalization of Jewish communal life and action have come together. This
same use of group dance as training to aid
community action has been discovered in our own
day in marches of movements for civil rights,
student rights, peace, etc. It is hoped that
this effort to outline the uses of dance will
increase the movement in many toward the uplift
of our world.

DANCING FOR REIDENTIFICATION
AND REDEDICATION TODAY

Adding movement to the singing of hymns in worship increases the sense of reidentification
with and rededication to the intentions of
Christianity. In chapter one, we noted a number
of such movements for use during recessional
hymns: taking the hands of others, moving to
the tripudium step, and turning around to face
the world while singing or actually moving out
of the church into the world were outlined.

Simply processing while singing a hymn may effect
increased identification. Processing through
the aisles of the church while singing "We Three
Kings" at Epiphany season led those who sang
the words to see themselves as kings, for the
people were actually doing what the lyrics
described. This identifying power can be used
to upgrade the people's evaluation of themselves
and their possibilities. On All Saints' Day
we assembled all the people outside the nave and
passed out children's instruments (rhythm
sticks, finger cymbal, tambourines, etc.) which
we had brought up from the kindergarten. Then
we processed into the nave and around the altar
while singing "When the Saints Go Marching In."
From the experience many went out expressing a
renewed commitment to living with a higher image
of themselves.

A most effective closing to worship combines a
meaningful gesture of benediction within the
context of a recessional use of the tripudium
step. [159] Through this dance, the people
sensed a heightening of community, repentance,
rejoicing and rededication. The choir began by

159. Dancers in my workshop at the Washington
Cathedral developed this sequence for worship
in February 1975.

repeatedly singing "Alleluia." Then they began
moving (with the tripudium step) around and
around the communion table as they continued
singing. They did not move in single file nor
in rows of two or three abreast with arms linked;
instead they moved as a massed group with each
person having a hand placed on a shoulder of one
person ahead of them. After they had moved
around the altar this way several times, they
invited others in the congregation to join them
as they continued to move in that pattern.
After a few more times around the altar, they
continued to sing "Alleluia" and move in a massed
group (with the tripudium step) up the stairs,
through the cathedral halls and outside into
the city.

APPENDIX I:

A SCHEMA OF OLD TESTAMENT TERMS FOR DANCE

SCRIPTURE PASSAGE	IN HEBREW	IN LXX GREEK	IN VULGATE LATIN
Judges 21.21; 21.23;	חול (chul)		
Psalm 30.11; 149.3; 150.4; Lam. 5.15; Jer. 31.4; 31.13;	מחול (mechol)	χορός	chorea
Ex. 15.20; 32.19; Judges 11.34; 21.21; I Sam. 18.6; 21.11; 29.5;	מחלה (mecholah)		
2 Sam. 6.14; 6.16;	כרר (karar)		
1 Ch. 15.29; Job 21.11; Eccl. 3.4; Isaiah 13.21;	רקד (raqad)	ὁρχουμενος	Saltatio

132

APPENDIX II: THE LORD'S PRAYER

All may be encouraged to engage in this choreography for the Lord's Prayer in the aisles or
in the chancel.   Those who choose not to dance
may sing whatever version is chosen.   As all
sing "Our Father who art in heaven, hallowed be
thy name," those who wish to dance could spread
their arms wide open and begin to move toward
others to form a circle or circles.   (Praying
"Our Father" should open us to the realization
that all people are our families.)   As all sing
"Thy Kingdom Come, Thy will be done, on earth
as it is in heaven," the dancers could come together in a moving circle or circles, join hands,
and uplift each others' arms.   (In this way we
realize that our hands are instruments for
bringing God's kingdom, that the kingdom is a
constantly moving one, and that we are not alone
in this endeavor: others' hands are involved
as well.)   As all sing "Give us this day our
daily bread," the dancers could kneel with hands
cupped before them in a posture of humbleness
(in recognition of our dependence); and as all
sing "and forgive us our debts," the dancers
could maintain their posture (which is one of
self-reflection on all that we have received in
our self-concern).   As all sing "as we forgive
our debtors," the dancers could begin to rise

and help others around them to rise (leaving
behind any thought of the past reflection and
self-preoccupation). As all sing "and lead us
not into temptation but deliver us from evil,"
the dancers who are now standing in a circle
could begin to move in a circle with their bodies
and arms held in such a way as to suggest the
rejection of the centrifugal force that would
destroy the circle. (Thus, we symbolize that
the community must continue moving in response
to God's command in order to avoid the infighting
that develops without such direction; and individuals must reject the temptation of evil
which attempts to tear the group apart.) Then
as all sing "for thine is the kingdom, and the
power, and the glory," the dancers may go off
in different directions and in diverse movements
symbolic of acts incarnating God's kingdom: one
or more may whirl in joy, two others may interact
to suggest some service or fellowship, etc.
(By these diverse actions, diversity is embraced
as part of the glory of God's kingdom.) Then
as all sing "forever and ever," all the dancers
could rush back together in a tight embrace
(to indicate our solidarity with all). And then
as all sing "Amen, Amen," the dancers could move
off boldly in different directions (for "Amen"
is a strong affirmation -- "so be it" -- and
should be symbolized by a going forth in faith.)

This version of the Lord's Prayer may be done before or after another danced version of the Lord's Prayer in a worship service. And then the people could be invited to discuss which danced version expressed their faith better. The advantage of dancing the Lord's Prayer two or more different ways on the same occasion is that it then encourages the people to think in terms of "which movements or which dances are most fitting" and "why" rather than to think they like or dislike "dance". And then the people could be asked to suggest other movements that might better express their faith and understanding of the Lord's Prayer.

A SELECT ANNOTATED BIBLIOGRAPHY

<u>FOR HISTORIC PERSPECTIVE</u>

HEBRAIC ROOTS

Lapson, Dvora, "Dance," <u>The Universal Jewish
    Encyclopedia</u> (New York, 1941), III, pp. 455-
    463. This article is the best short survey
    of Hebrew dancing through all periods.

Oesterley, W.O.E., <u>The Sacred Dance</u>, (New York,
    1923). This volume is still the best
    examination of dance in Old Testament terms
    and cultural settings. (Available in paper-
    back for $3.95 from Dance Horizons Inc.)
    More recent investigations into the Sumero-
    Accadian milieu alter Oesterley's evalua-
    tions of the continuity and distinctiveness
    of Hebraic dances. (Cf. Alfred Haldar,
    <u>Associations of Cult Prophets Among the
    Ancient Semites</u>, (Uppsala, 1945).

Morgenstern, Julian, "The Etymological History
    of the Three Hebrew Synonyms for "To Dance'",
    <u>American Oriental Society Journal</u>, 36,
    (1916), pp. 321-332.
    This is the best word study of Old Testament
    terminology for dance and yields the insight
    that Hebrew dance is intimately connected
    with the active use of the material world
    and certainly not any other worldly
    activity.

Fisher, Constance, <u>Dancing The Old Testament:
    Christian Celebrations of Israelite Heritage
    For Worship and Education</u> (Austin, 1980).
    Translates old testament dances by percept-
    ively using folk dance forms of today.
    $5.95 from the Sharing Company.

GREEK ROOTS

Lawler, Lillian, The Dance in Ancient Greece,
    (Middleton, 1964). This volume is the
    definitive one on the subject. (Available
    in hardcover for $2.95 from the Dance Mart.)

THE CHRISTIAN CHURCH

Backman, E. Louis, Religious Dances in the
    Christian Church and in Popular Medicine,
    (London, 1952). A cataloguing of material
    translated from early church through nine-
    teenth century sources.

Taylor, Margaret Fisk, A Time To Dance: Symbolic
    Movement in Worship, (Austin, 1980).
    This volume is a readily available intro-
    duction to Dance in Christian Worship.
    Twentieth century developments and resources
    are detailed as well as materials listed in
    Backman. Many fine illustrations from Art
    Collections. (Available in paperback for
    $5.95 from The Sharing Co., P. O. Box 2224,
    Austin, Texas 78768-2224.)

FOR CONGREGATIONAL PARTICIPATION

Adams, Doug, Involving the People in Dancing
    Worship: Historic and Contemporary Patterns.
    This booklet contains all that one needs to
    know to reenact historic church services
    with dance (order of worship and other
    details as well as dance steps for early
    church, medieval, Orthodox, Early American
    and Nineteenth Century American reenact-
    ments.) Available in paperback from The

Sharing Co.. P. O. Box 2224, Austin, Texas
78768-2224. $2.00 per copy.

_____, "The Chagall Windows as Chore-
ography: Stained Glass as Inspiration for
Dance In Worship," Stained Glass, Spring,
Summer 1974, Vol. 69, No. 1-2, pp. 4-7.
Discusses how a dance choir and congregation
may inspire the movement of their worship
by looking to their stained glass and other
art. $1.25 from The Sharing Company

_____, Dancing Christmas Carols sets some
30 carols to dance in folk dance forms.
$6.95 from The Sharing Company.

_____, "Affirming Diversity in Liturgical
Dance," Modern Liturgy, March 1977, Vol. 4,
No. 3. This entire issue is edited by Doug
Adams and devoted to dance in worship with
articles by Adelaide Ortegl, Margaret
Taylor, Carla DeSola, John Moss, and others.
$3.00 per copy from The Sharing Company.

DeSola, Carla, The Spirit Moves: Dance In Worship
and Prayers, Washington D.C., 1977. The
Liturgical Conference. This volume combines
most of Carla DeSola's columns on the use
of dance for the people in worship that
have appeared in Liturgy. "Congregations
and Gestures," Liturgy, March 1974, Vol. 19,
No. 3, pp. 9-13. Gives many valuable
suggestions for people's movements at moments of the Catholic Mass. This entire
issue of Liturgy is devoted to dance in
worship. Available at $2.00 per copy from
The Liturgical Conference, 1330 Massachusetts
Ave., N.W., Washington, D.C., 20005. Her book
The Spirit Moves is $9.95 from Sharing Company.

Taylor, Margaret Fisk, Creative Movement: Steps
    Toward Understanding, (New York, 1969).
    This pamphlet is the first to present
    suggestions for congregational dance. A
    half dozen such choreographies are detailed.
    Available for $2.00 from The Sharing Co.,
    P. O. Box 2224, Austin, Texas, 78767.

_____, Dramatic Dance With Children In
    Education and Worship. This workbook and
    others by Margaret Taylor give choreographies
    for children; but these may be easily
    adapted for congregational participation.
    (Available for $4.95 from The Sharing Co.,
    P. O. Box 2224, Austin, Texas, 78767.

_____, Look Up and Live: Dance in Prayer,
    $4.95 from The Sharing Company.

Bruce, Violet, and Tooke, Joan, Lord of the
    Dance: An Approach to Religious Education,
    (London, 1966). Much material here is also
    adaptable for congregational movement.

Emery, Lynne Fauley, "Sacred Dance," Black Dance
    in the United States From 1619 to 1970.
    Finally we have a definitive book on black
    dance. And pp. 119-138 provide excellent
    descriptions of dance in Southern black
    worship.

Johnson, Charles, The Frontier Camp Meeting.
    This definitive book on camp meeting worship
    in nineteenth century America provides much
    on the marching out song. (c.f. pp. 41-47,
    57-61, 122-144.)

Andrews, Edward, The Gift to be Simple, (New York, 1940). This volume contains all details on the songs and choreographies of the Shakers. Shaker theology is at variance with Christianity at several points (the celebate Shakers, who looked upon the body as evil in certain respects, devised dance steps that restrain rather than liberate and make some of their dances into anti-incarnational events), but the tunes and movements are suggestive for organization of congregational movement. Lyrics may be changed to express fully Christian faith: "Lord of the Dance" by Sydney Carter is a new lyric to the old Shaker tune "Gift to be Simple."

Ortegel, Adelaide, A Dancing People, (West Lafayette, 1976). Profusely illustrated with particularly helpful suggestions on using folk dance and other folk ways in worship. $6.95 from The Sharing Company.

Sacred Dance Guild Journal, a quarterly, compiles and details the dance activity church by church. All conferences and publications are announced and resource people in each area listed. This is the invaluable resource as each issue will provide fifty or sixty ideas for worship services. (Subscribe through The Sacred Dance Guild, c/o Susan Cole, 3917 N.E. 44St. Vancouver, Washington 98661. $16 per year but $8 for students.)

Trolin, Clifford, Movement In Prayer In A Hasidic Mode (Austin, 1979). Vigorous movement expands prayer. $2.50 from The Sharing Company.

140

Dance Magazine is the best secular publication
and the only one indexed in Reader's Guide
to Periodicals. Articles on movement in
church occasionally appear. $18.00 per year
from Danad Publishing Co., 10 Columbus
circle. New York. New York 10019.

FOR THEOLOGICAL UNDERSTANDING

Buber, Martin, "Spirit and Body of the Hasidic
Movement," The Origin and Meaning of
Hasidism, (New York, 1966), pp. 114-149.
From this book and Morgenstern's article
mentioned earlier, one can gain a good
understanding of the theology underlying
Hebraic dance. See also Buber's chapter
on "Symbolic and Sacramental Existence."

Allchin, A. H., ed., Sacrament and Image (London,
1967). This volume contains the best
Eastern Orthodox exposition of incarnational
theology as a basis for dance. (Available
for $1.05 from the Society of St. Albins
and St. Sergius, The Book Room, St. Basil's
House, 52 Ladbroke Grove, London, W.11,
England.)

Knox, Ronald, The Mass In Slow Motion, (New York,
1948). The best Roman Catholic description
of the mass as dance, although Hugo Rahner's
book Man at Play gives a good Catholic
basis for more active dance as we see
ourselves in his terms as God's body.

Adams, Doug and Rock, Judith, Biblical Criteria
In Modern Dance: Modern Dance As A Prophetic
Form (Austin, 1979). Given at the 1979
Jerusalem Seminar on The Bible In Dance.
$2.50 from The Sharing Company.

Robinson, John A. T., The Body: A Study in Pauline Theology, (London, 1952). The best Western exposition of incarnational theology which corrects the meaning of "spirit" and "flesh" and thus provides a basis to encourage rather than discourage dance.

Cox, Harvey, Feast of Fools, (Boston, 1969). A good chapter explains the social action significance of dance in terms of the gaining of the vision that the present social order is not absolute.

Cleaver, Eldridge, Soul On Ice, (New York, 1968). An evaluation of American culture which compellingly argues for the social action significance of dance to move the American soul off ice and into action.

FOR PURCHASING MATERIALS

Dance Horizon Books, 1801 East 26th St., Brooklyn, New York, 11229; Dance Mart, Box 48, Homecrest Station, Brooklyn, New York, 11229; Resource Publications, P.O.Box 444, Saratoga Calif. 95070; The Sharing Company, P. O. Box 2224, Austin, Texas, 78768-2224.

ADDENDA

Rock, Judith, Theology In The Shape Of Dance: Dance In Worship and Theological Process (Austin, 1977). A vital guide for the leaders of worship and dance groups to develop stronger dance. $2.50 from The Sharing Company.

BIBLIOGRAPHY

Abrahams, Israel, Jewish Life in the Middle Ages, New York, 1896, Macmillan Co.

Adams, Doug, Congregational Dancing In Christian Worship, Aurora, 1976, The Sharing Company.

_____, Involving The People In Dancing Worship: Historic and Contemporary Patterns, Grand Rapids, 1975, The Sacred Dance Guild.

_____, "The Chagall Windows as Choreography: Stained Glass as Inspiration for Dance In Worship," Stained Glass, Spring-Summer 1974, Vol. 69, No. 1-2, pp 4-7.

_____, "Affirming Diversity in Liturgical Dance," Modern Liturgy, March 1977, Vol. 4, No. 3.

Aker, Suzanna, "To Carol Is To Dance," Dance Magazine, December 1964, pp. 40-41.

Allchin, A. M., ed., Sacrament and Image, London, 1967. Fellowship of S. Alban and S. Sergius.

Anderson, Jack, "Ferment and Controversy," Dance Magazine, August 1969, XLIII, 8, pp. 47-55.

Arnold, Thomas, ed., Selected Works, Oxford, 1869, B. Fellows.

Attwater, D., ed., A Catholic Dictionary, New York, 1962, Macmillan Co.

Augustine, "Exposition of Psalms, " The Nicene and Post Nicene Fathers, first series, 8, New York, 1888.

Backman, E. Louis, Religious Dances in the Christian Church and Popular Medicine, London, 1952, Allen and Unwin.

Benson, Robert Hugh, Papers of A Pariah, London, 1909, Longmans, Green and Co.

Berk, Fred, ed., The Jewish Dance, New York, 1960, Exposition Press.

Black, Matthew, The Aramaic Approach to the Gospels and Acts, London, 1967, Clarendon Press.

Bonifazi, Conrad, A Theology of Things, Philadelphia, 1967, Lippincott.

Braude, William G., trans., The Midrash on Psalms, New Haven, 1959, Yale University Press.

Bruce, Violet, and Tooke, Joan, Lord of the Dance: An Approach to Religious Education, London, 1966, Pergamon Press.

Canner, Norma, And A Time To Dance, Boston, 1968, Beacon Press.

Carawan, Guy, ed., We Shall Overcome: Songs of the Southern Freedom Movement, New York, 1963, Oak Pub.

Carr, William, trans., General Instruction of the Roman Missal, Quincy, Illinois, 1969.

Cleaver, Eldridge, Soul on Ice, New York, 1968, McGraw Hill.

Colson, F. H., trans., "The Contemplative Life," Philo, IX, pp. 104-169, Cambridge, 1954.

Conybeare, Fred C., Philo About the Contemplative Life, Oxford, 1895.

Cox, Harvey, The Feast of Fools, New York, 1969.

Creative Arts in Reconciliation, New York, 1969, Friendship Press.

"Dancing," The Catholic Encyclopedia, New York, 1908, Robert Appleton Co.

Davies, G. Horton, "Dancing," The Interpreter's Dictionary of the Bible, Nashville, 1956.

Delling, Gerhard, "Prayer," Worship in the New Testament, London, 1963, Darton, Longman, and Todd.

De Sola, Carla, The Spirit Moves: Dance In Worship and Prayer, Washington D.C., 1977, The Liturgical Conference.

Ellis, Havelock, The Dance of Life, New York, 1923, Riverside Press.

Epstein, I., ed., The Talmud, London, 1938, Soncino Press.

Eusebius, The Ecclesiastical History and the Martyrs of Palestine, H. J. Lawlor, D.E.L. Oulton, ed., London.

Freedman, H., and Simon, Maurice, ed., The Midrash, London, 1939, Sencino Press.

Freehof, Florence, Jews Are A Dancing People, San Francisco, 1954, Stark-Rath.

Ginzberg, Louis, The Legends of the Jews, Philadelphia, 1938, The Jewish Publication Society of America.

Gordon, Cyrus, "David the Dancer," Yehezkel Kaufmann Jubilee Volume, pp. 46-49, Jerusalem, 1960, Hebrew University Press.

Haldar, Alfred, Associations of Cult Prophets Among the Ancient Semites, Uppsala, 1945, Almquist and Wiksells.

Harrison, G. B., ed., Shakespeare, Major Plays, New York, 1948, Harcourt Brace Co.

Hertzberg, Hans, I and II Samuel: A Commentary, Philadelphia, 1968, Westminster Press.

Hirsch, Emil G., "Dance: The Biblical Data,"
    The Jewish Encyclopedia, Isadore Singer,
    ed., New York, 1903.

Hymnal For Young Christians, Chicago, 1968,
    F. E. L. Pub.

Jackson, Samuel, "Dancing," The Schaff-Herzog
    Encyclopedia of Religious Knowledge, (New
    York, 1908).

Johnson, Aubrey, "The Role of the King in the
    Jerusalem Cultus," The Labyrinth, S. H.
    Hooke, ed., London, 1935.

_____, The Vitality of the Individual
    in the Thought of Ancient Israel, Cardiff,
    1949, University of Wales Press.

Knox, Ronald, The Mass In Slow Motion, New York,
    1948, Sheed and Ward.

Lawler, Lillian, The Dance in Ancient Greece,
    Middleton, 1964.

Leeuw, Gerhardus van der, Sacred and Profane
    Beauty: the Holy in Art, New York, 1963,
    Holt Rinehart & Winston.

Loewe, H., Rabinic Anthology, New York, 1938,
    Meridian Books.

Lossky, Vladimar, The Mystical Theology of the
    Eastern Church, London, 1957, James Clarke
    & Co.

Maritain, Jacques, Art and Scholasticism, trans.
    J. F. Scanlow, New York, 1930, Scribner.

Marshall, J. T., Manual of the Aramaic Language
    of the Palestinian Talmud, Leyden, 1929,
    E. J. Brill Ltd.

Mead, G. R., The Sacred Dance in Christendom,
    "Quest Reprint Series," N. 2, London,
    1926, J. M. Watkins.

Menestrier, Des Ballets Anciens et Modernes,
    Paris, 1682.

Migne, ed., Patrologia Graeca, Paris, 1857.

_____, Patrologia Latina, Paris, 1857.

Morgenstern, Julian, "The Etymological History
    of Three Hebrew Synonyms for 'To Dance,'"
    American Oriental Society Journal, 36,
    1916, pp. 321-332.

Newman, Louis I., The Hasidic Anthology, New
    York, 1934, Block Pub. Co.

Oesterley, W. O. E., The Sacred Dance, New York,
    1923, Dance Horizons.

Ortegal, Adelaide, A Dancing People, West
    Lafayette, 1976, Center For Contemporary
    Celebration.

Pilgrim Hymnal, Boston, 1964, The Pilgrim Press.

Polanyi, Michael, Personal Knowledge: Towards A
    Post-Critical Philosophy, New York, 1964,
    Harper & Row.

Porter, J. R., "An Interpretation of II Samuel
    VI and Psalm CXXXII," The Journal of Theo-
    logical Studies, V, 1954, pp. 161-173.

Poston, Elizabeth, The Penguin Book of Christmas
    Carols, London, 1965, Lowe and Brydone.

Repp, Ray, "Songs From Come Alive," F. E. L.
    Songbook IV, Chicago, 1967, F. E. L.
    Publications.

Rey, C. F., The Real Abyssinia, London, n.d.

Robinson, John A. T., The Body: A Study in
    Pauline Theology, London, 1963, SCM Press.

Roth, Cecil, The Jews in the Renaissance,
    Philadelphia, 1964, Jewish Publication
    Society of America.

Sahlin, M., Etude sur la carole medieval,
    Uppsala, 1940.

Sandys, W., Carols Ancient and Modern, London,
    1833.

Schecter, S., ed., Aboth de Rabbi Nathan,
    London, 1887.

Schutz, C., Joy: Expanding Human Awareness, New York, 1967, Grove Press.

Sewell, Elizabeth, The Orphic Voice: Poetry and Natural History, London, 1961, Routledge and Kegan Paul.

Shawn, Ted, "Religious Use of Dance, " Religious Symbolism, Frederick Johnson, ed., New York, 1955, Harper & Row.

Sinclair, John, trans., The Divine Comedy of Dante Alighieri, New York, 1961, Oxford University Press.

Smith, William Robertson, Lectures on the Religion of the Semites, London, 1914.

Sorell, Walter, The Dance Through the Ages, New York, 1967, Grosset and Dunlap.

Strack, Hermann L., Introduction to the Talmud and Midrash, Philadelphia, 1931.

Taylor, Margaret Fisk, A Time to Dance: Symbolic Movement in Worship, Austin, 1976, The Sharing Company.

_____, Creative Movement: Steps Towards Understanding, New York, 1969, Friendship Press.

_____ Dramatic Dance With Children In Education and Worship, Austin, 1976, The Sharing Company.

150

_____, Look Up and Live: Dance in Prayer, Austin, 1976, The Sharing Company.

Temple, William, Nature, Man and God, London, 1935.

Toy, C. H., "The Meaning of Pesach," Journal of Biblical Literature, XVI, (1897), pp. 178-179.

Underhill, Evelyn, Eucharistic Prayers From Ancient Liturgies, London, 1939.

_____, Worship, New York, 1957, Harper & Row.

Vaux, R. de, Ancient Israel, New York, 1961.

Williams, Vaughan, The Oxford Book of Carols, London, 1928.

Winward, S. F., The Reformation of Our Worship, Richmond, 1964.

Zernov, Nicholas, Eastern Orthodoxy, London, 1961, Weidenfeld & Nicholson.

_____, Orthodox Encounter, London, 1961, James Clarke & Co. Ltd.

151

INDEX

154

A TIME TO DANCE:
SYMBOLIC MOVEMENT IN WORSHIP
*(1976 revised edition, 192pp.)

First of all, *A TIME TO DANCE* is a "how to" book. It tells graphically and step-by-step how to be a leader of a dance choir, how many members to have, ways to dress, light, and stage the dance, and trickiest of all how to get men and boys to join the group. There are descriptions of dance dramas, processions, narrative outlines, and special programs for religious holidays.

A fascinating section on the history of religious dance begins with the biblical "David danced before the Lord with all his might" and continues through the early church and medieval period. A third section brings to life the renaissance of dance movement in twentieth century religious worship.

by Margaret Taylor $5.95 per copy

DRAMATIC DANCE WITH CHILDREN
IN EDUCATION AND WORSHIP
(1976 edition, 96pp.)

This book might be titled "How to use creative dramatic movement in Christian education." It is **addressed especially to the church school teacher and parents of children five through eleven.** (But the ideas are adaptable for older youth as well.) Drawing on the best parts of *TIME FOR DISCOVERY* and *TIME FOR WONDER* she tells how movement can be used **to create a new climate in which children discover more about themselves and others, the world, and the Creator.** Interpretations of biblical stories, parables, hymns, Christmas and Easter carols, the Lord's Prayer, and folk games are given; but the author stresses that these are only starting points. She encourages leaders to do their own experiments and to let children develop their own interpretations.

by Margaret Taylor $4.95 per copy

The books listed on this and the following page can be purchased for the amount specified from The Sharing Co., P. O. Box 2224, Austin, TX 78767. Make checks payable to The Sharing Co. Add 50¢ per book for postage.

LOOK UP AND LIVE:
(DANCE IN PRAYER AND MEDITATION)
(1976 edition, 96pp.)

This book responds to the needs for body, mind, and soul to work cooperatively helping individuals to meet life with less tension and with more strength, with less discouragement and with more joy. Of the numerous movements described, all are appropriate in facilitating lives of **personal prayer and meditation;** but **a number of these movements may be used in corporate prayer** and worship. Although the attention in this book is to helping **adults discover more vibrant forms of prayer and meditation,** the methods are useful with youth in education as well.

These movements to hymns may be used for the whole congregation in worship or by a dance choir to develop choreography for worship; or the movements **may simply be done by the individual in developing his or her own life** through these incarnating ways of prayer.

by Margaret Taylor $4.95 per copy

CREATIVE MOVEMENT:
STEPS TOWARDS UNDERSTANDING
(Reconciliation In Groups)
(1969 edition, 12pp.)

Understanding that **dramatic movement is a basic and natural way of communication.** Margaret Fisk Taylor shows how it can be used as a form of group dynamics **for greater clarification and understanding.**

Explains individual, pairs, and group participation in an easy to follow form from beginning movements to more complex forms. Gives direction in movement to spoken words, music without words, and vocal music. **Shows involvement of family relationships and generation relationships** along with topics for exploration within these frameworks. **Particularly effective in involving children.** Explains how there is rejoicing in the excitement of new inter-relationships showing how true reconciliation leads into celebration.

Gives examples using The Lord's Prayer, **No Man Is An Island,** The Doxology, **You Can Tell The World, What The World Needs Now, Rise Up O Men of God,** and **God of Grace and God of Glory.**

by Margaret Taylor $2.00 per copy

DANCING CHRISTMAS CAROLS
edited by Doug Adams

with members of the Sacred Dance Guild of the United States and Canada

Dancing Christmas Carols is a sourcebook of ideas for carolers of all ages and kinds, with examples for adding movement and gestures to:
- holiday social events
- street caroling
- children's Christmas parties
- family fun
- community gatherings
- classroom programs
- Christmas worship

The movements range from many very simple gestures through sophisticated jazz and modern dance steps. Illustrated with diagrams and photographs.

134 pages, paper,   **$6.95**
ISBN 0-89390-006-0

"This book puts together song and dance, the two great universal languages, in a season that unites in spirit people of all ages, beliefs, languages, temperaments and abilities."

Sr. Dianna Vossen, OSB
St. Benedict's Convent
St. Joseph, MN
SISTERS TODAY Magazine

Contents
Foreword

158

Other boo_____through
The Shari_____24, Austin,
Texas, 78_____ck for
total amount plus $1 for postage and
handling.)

Adams, Doug, <u>Congregational Dancing In Christian Worship</u>, $4.95
  1984 expanded edition, 161 pp.
Adams, Doug, Dancing Christmas Carols (1978, 132 pp.) **$6**.95
Adams, Doug, <u>Involving The People In Dancing Worship:</u>
  <u>Historic and Contemporary Patterns</u> (1977, 21pp.) **$2.00**
Adams, Doug, "The Chagall Windows As Choreography:
  Stained Glass As Inspiration For Dance" (1974) $1.25
Adams, Doug, "Vitalizing Worship With Dance" (1979) $1.75
Adams, Doug, "Dancing The Seasons" (1979) $1.25

Bellamak, Lu, <u>Non-Judgemental Sacred Dance: Simple Ways</u>
  <u>To Pray Through Dance</u> (1978, 23 pp.) $2.50
DeSola, Carla, <u>The Spirit Moves: A Handbook of Dance</u>
  <u>For Prayer</u> (1977, 169 pp.) $9.95
Reed, Carlynn, <u>And We Have Danced: The History of The</u>
  <u>Sacred Dance Guild, 1958 - 1978</u> (1978, 202 pp.) $5.95
Rock, Judith, <u>Theology In The Shape of Dance: Using</u>
  <u>Dance In Worship and Theological Process</u> (27 pp.) **$2.50**
Rock, Judith, and Adams, Doug, <u>Biblical Criteria In</u>
  <u>Modern Dance: Modern Dance As A Prophetic Form</u>(1979) $2.50
Seaton, Linda Kahn, <u>Scriptural Choreography: Biblical</u>
  <u>Dance Forms In Shaping Contemporary Worship</u> (1979) $2.50
Taussig, Hal, <u>Dancing The New Testament: A Guide To</u>
  <u>Texts for Movement</u> (1977, 12 pp.) $2.00
Taylor, Margaret, <u>Considerations For Starting and</u>
  <u>Stretching A Sacred Dance Choir</u> (1978, 36 pp.) $2.75
Taylor, Margaret, <u>Creative Movement: Steps Toward</u>
  <u>Understanding</u> (1969, 12 pp.) $2.00
Taylor, Margaret, <u>Dramatic Dance With Children In</u>
  <u>Worship and Education</u> (1977, 96 pp.) $4.95
Taylor, Margaret, <u>Look Up and Live: Dance In Prayer</u>
  <u>and Meditation</u> (1977, 96 pp.) $4.95
Taylor, Margaret, <u>A Time To Dance: Symbolic Movement</u>
  <u>In Worship</u> (1976 revised edition, 192 pp.) $5.95
Trolin, Clifford, <u>Movement In Prayer In A Hasidic</u>
  <u>Mold</u> (1979, 14 pp.) $2.50
Fisher, Constance, <u>Dancing The Old Testament: Chris-</u>
  <u>tian Celebrations of Israelite Heritage For Worship</u>
  <u>and Education</u> (1980, 128 pp.) $5.95